T0327478

INVESTING IN ENERGY

Since 1996, Bloomberg Press has published books for financial professionals on investing, economics, and policy affecting investors. Titles are written by leading practitioners and authorities, and have been translated into more than 20 languages.

The Bloomberg Financial Series provides both core reference knowledge and actionable information for financial professionals. The books are written by experts familiar with the work flows, challenges, and demands of investment professionals who trade the markets, manage money, and analyze investments in their capacity of growing and protecting wealth, hedging risk, and generating revenue.

For a list of available titles, please visit our web site at www.wiley.com/go/bloombergpress.

INVESTING IN ENERGY

A Primer on the Economics of
the Energy Industry

Gianna Bern

BLOOMBERG PRESS
An Imprint of
WILEY

Published by John Wiley & Sons, Inc., Hoboken, New Jersey.
Published simultaneously in Canada.

For general information on our other products and services or for technical support, please contact our Customer Care Department within the United States at (800) 762-2974, outside the United States at (317) 572-3993, or fax (317) 572-4002.

Wiley also publishes its books in a variety of electronic formats. Some content that appears in print may not be available in electronic books. For more information about Wiley products, visit our web site at www.wiley.com.

Library of Congress Cataloging-in-Publication Data:

Bern, Gianna.
  Investing in energy : a primer on the economics of the energy industry / Gianna Bern.
      p.   cm. – (Bloomberg financial series)
  Includes index.
  ISBN 978-1-57660-375-8 (hardback); ISBN 978-0-47087-878-1 (ebk);
  978-1-118-12838-1 (ebk); 978-1-118-12839-8 (ebk)
  1. Energy industries–Finance.   2. Investments.   I. Title.
  HD9502.A2B475 2011
  333.79–dc22   2011006383

Printed in the United States of America

10   9   8   7   6   5   4   3   2   1

This book is dedicated to my incredible family whose encouragement eradicated any doubt that this project was achievable: my treasured parents, my sister, brother, and their spouses, and my husband and children, who have lovingly nurtured and sustained the heart and soul of this budding author. Thank you all for your support, patience, and understanding.

Contents

Preface

It is my sincere hope that this book lays a foundation for those new to energy and fills in gaps for the veterans of the energy sector. The energy sector is a very complex and growing sector for investment. *Investing in Energy* illustrates numerous developments worthy of consideration and review by those interested in learning more about and investing in energy.

This book takes a comprehensive and financial approach to learning about oil, gas, and renewable energy. Part I reviews financial considerations necessary for evaluating and assessing cash flow, capital structure, and the role of capital markets across a myriad of energy sector firms.

Part II is the heart of the book and covers the economics inherent to the oil and gas sector such as reserves, production, crack spreads, and refining economics. We also review certain basics relevant to the oil and gas markets and explore why the crude oil and natural gas markets behave the way they do. Part II considers the role of OPEC, production rights, oilfield sector companies, oil juniors, independent oil companies, and national oil companies. Finally, Part II evaluates the complex landscape of crude oil pricing and its volatility in the commodity markets.

Part III of *Investing in Energy* assesses the current state of the power sector across various global markets. In this section, we bring readers up to date on developments in solar energy, hydro electrical power, nuclear power, geothermal electricity, and wind energy.

Part IV addresses developments in green energy such as bio fuels and ethanol. Once again, we analyze various other global markets, to ascertain where there are challenges and perhaps some opportunities across the energy landscape for biofuels, biomass, and ethanol.

Part V concludes with a summary of various opportunities we explored in the book and reviews the notion of energy policy as a sovereign's strategic and economic imperative.

Acknowledgments

Books are rarely the efforts of a single individual. I must acknowledge the incredible assistance from my husband and business partner Lester Bern, whose insights, advice, and editorial assistance are pervasive throughout this book. He kept my feet to the fire, always insisting upon perfection; this book would not have been possible without his help. I would also like to acknowledge my appreciation for Lester's technical and editorial expertise in chapters 16–19.

Enormous gratitude also goes to my outstanding editorial team at John Wiley & Sons: Laura Walsh, senior editor, and Judy Howarth, development editor. Their guidance and editorial expertise were indeed extraordinary and valuable. I am fortunate that they were on my team. Thanks are also given to the Wiley graphics department for its creative expertise and to my production editor, Melissa Lopez for her insights and patience.

Special acknowledgements and thanks are given to Team Pope for its unique analytics and graphics assistance.

My colleagues at Capital IQ and Bloomberg News are thanked for permitting me to use, throughout the book, various proprietary data used for illustrative purposes.

Special thanks go to Evan Barton, the Bloomberg Press editor who recognized the merits of this project and championed it in its early days. This book would not have been possible without his initial support. Finally, another special heartfelt thank you is extended to Joe Carroll of Bloomberg News, for his early and continuing support of this project.

INVESTING IN
ENERGY

PART I

Introduction and Financial Considerations

1

CHAPTER 1

Historical Perspectives

The energy industry is undergoing unprecedented change as it reacts to new challenges in safety, regulation, exploration, and alternative-energy initiatives. One need only layer on the global political environment and the long-ranging repercussions of the 2010 Gulf of Mexico oil spill or the turmoil in the Middle East to realize that the energy sector is as complex as it has ever been. From this increasing complexity springs the need for this book. The following pages present a framework for understanding the basic elements of energy-industry economics. While not covering geology or refining from technical standpoints, this book provides a framework for analyzing the industry's basics and economics, and thereby helps prepare investors and other energy-industry professionals to more confidently venture forth into this vast and complex sector.

This book explores various opportunities available to investors in the energy arena and provides tools to better equip those new and not so new to investing in oil, gas, and alternatively generated energy. Time-tested analytic tools and investment criteria are utilized to provide the reader a better understanding of the economics behind the various energy sectors. Thoughtful and deliberate use of these analytic tools should enable deeper understandings of opportunities and more confident investment decisions. Also, long after the scent of fresh ink and paper have faded, we hope that this book will remain a trusted reference on many facets of commercial energy markets.

Chapter 1 explores some of the issues of the day in energy and places it in a historical context. We also review some of the key issues such as production and reserve growth for oil and gas producers. Cost structures continue to be a key consideration for alternative energy producers as project sponsors grapple with reducing electricity costs to become more competitive with that of fossil fuel producers. Next, we layer in the challenges in the regulatory environment that affect all energy producers. This chapter sets the foundation on which the next 21 chapters will build.

3

Oil and Gas Producers

A term that is used often in this book is *integrated major* (or major). This term refers to the industry business model of a large, vertically integrated oil and gas producer that has upstream, midstream, and downstream operations. Upstream refers to exploration and production, midstream consists of storage and transport, downstream refers to refining and retail operations. For integrated majors, the road ahead is one marked with significant challenges. In the wake of maturing basins, integrated majors are faced with stable to decreasing crude oil and natural gas production. The majors are also faced with the challenges associated with increasing crude oil and natural gas reserves in an environment where the preponderance of global reserves are controlled by national governments. The era of easy oil has indeed ended and the global oil industry is equally challenged by the development of new forms of alternative energies to meet future energy demand.

For national oil companies, the situation is different, but improving. National oil companies are challenged to extract hydrocarbons in an economical manner while supplying revenues to their governments. Therein lays the dichotomy and challenge. National oil companies are perennially faced with providing for the vast majority of their home country's economic resources. Many small national oil companies face a more precarious position of having to continually depend on high crude oil prices.

Are high crude oil prices a phenomenon of the past? While none of us has a crystal ball, the market consensus is that demand for crude and its refined products is going nowhere but up. Therefore, high crude oil prices have returned with a vengeance. How high is high? Over the near term, triple digit crude prices have returned but may not be sustainable over the longer term. The wild card is global economic recovery and returning crude oil demand from the 34-member Organization for Economic Co-operation and Development (OECD) countries. Currently, emerging market economies of China, India, Brazil, and Indonesia are contributing to the growth in crude and natural gas markets. Moreover, these emerging markets are stabilizing crude oil prices and preventing downward pricing pressure.

The natural gas market is currently in a pricing downturn. However, if we look beyond natural gas prices, we see a natural gas sector poised for future growth. Currently, natural gas inventories remain at relatively high levels contributing to the downward pressure on pricing. Natural gas is quickly becoming the fuel of choice as consumers and industries seek to move to greener solutions. Natural gas is becoming the fuel of choice because it is the *cleaner fuel*.

Moreover, unconventional natural gas shales (described more fully in Chapter 8) in the United States are in an unprecedented boom. Producers are seeking to acquire acreage in the U.S. basins of the Marcellus, Bakken, Eagle Ford, Haynesville, and Barnett Shale unconventional natural gas shale plays. According to the U.S. Department of Energy, growth in the U.S. natural gas market has the propensity to increase proven U.S. natural gas reserves almost three-fold over the next decade as producers aggressively move to categorize unconventional shale gas deposits as proved reserves (see Chapter 6). At the same time, development of these unconventional natural gas shales will have a weakening effect on natural gas prices as new supply comes on-line. The U.S. Department of Energy and producers believe that demand for natural gas will continue to increase over the next decade because of its attractiveness as a clean-burning and attractively-priced fuel. While natural gas continues to grow in the United States, it is a much quieter story outside of the United States.

Production Perspectives

Integrated majors are looking beyond the once-prolific basins of the North Sea and Cantarell in the Gulf of Mexico, or shallower waters of the Gulf of Mexico. Today, the oil and gas industry is exploring in the Arctic Circle, off the west coast of Africa, and in the deep waters of the South Atlantic. The industry is exploring where the engineering and logistical challenges are significant. The engineering feats necessary to explore, develop, and transport fuels in $-20°F$ ($-29°C$) are not insignificant.

This doesn't consider the costs associated with drilling in harsh environmental conditions. For novices to energy, exploration and production (E&P) represent the single biggest expense to oil and gas companies. Conversely, the E&P side of the business produces the largest portion of the revenues.

Today, most oil and gas production companies face significant production challenges. As basins mature, the integrated majors are not only left to explore in harsh environments but they are in the midst of stable to declining production profiles. Why is that? Independent oil companies do not own most of the oil and gas reserves on the planet. In most countries, governments own the mineral rights associated with oil or gas deposits. The oil and gas laws and regulations vary with each country.

Safety in Deepwater Drilling

Rig workers perform incredibly dangerous work, often in harsh working conditions. Included in the harsh environment is the practice of deepwater drilling. In April 2010, the Transocean-owned Deepwater Horizon platform exploded in the U.S. Gulf of Mexico killing 11 rig workers. Television news programs broadcast the challenges—reminiscent of NASA spacewalks and planetary rovers—of maneuvering heavy equipment in the 5,000 foot-deep waters of the Gulf of Mexico. The world watched as BP p.l.c. (BP) engineers finally capped and plugged the infamous runaway Macondo well in what became the worst oil spill in U.S. history.

The BP oil spill resulted in numerous countries reviewing safety standards and emergency response systems. There is no doubt that renewed or enhanced safety precautions, standards, and emergency response measures are necessary, particularly in deep water-drilling situations.

One of the oil and gas industry's responses to the BP spill was forming and implementing a collective effort to build a containment system to capture oil spilling in deepwater situations. An ExxonMobil-led consortium was formed to respond to such deep water-drilling emergencies. Consortium members, including Shell, Chevron, and Conoco Philips, each contributed US$250 million to form the joint-venture corporation. We believe that industry-led initiatives aimed at enhancing safety will continue to be put forth.

As authorities continue to sort through the details of this tragic accident, the industry and regulators must take steps to prevent these catastrophes, on behalf of employees, the environment, and regional economies. However, the collateral damage in the industry will be felt for years as sovereigns, municipalities, states, and provinces all over the globe assess deepwater drilling.

One of the most significant repercussions is that of increased regulation of deepwater drilling. Many sovereign nations are reassessing their current safety policies and those of the companies drilling in their waters. Included in this is a review of emergency response systems and the infrastructure necessary to manage a catastrophic drilling event.

Regulators around the globe also have tightened up the process of leasing and permitting new deepwater wells. The U.S. reaction to the oil spill has been to implement a moratorium, shutting down all new deepwater drilling projects. As of this writing, we still do not have an independent assessment of the accident. And while drilling officially reopened in the Gulf of Mexico, to date few drilling permits have been issued.

Many sovereign nations are pursuing deepwater drilling despite the risks. For many countries, deepwater drilling represents economic opportunity and badly needed revenues. By shutting down deepwater drilling, these countries would pay an unacceptable economic price. The best example of this is Brazil. There will be more on Brazil in Chapter 2, Investment Opportunities in Energy.

Importance of Reserves

One of the more significant challenges for an independent oil company (IOC) is growing its reserve base. In Chapter 6, we will review the industry standards for measuring and determining hydrocarbon reserves. Growing the reserve base becomes increasingly complex when one considers that virtually 80 percent of global reserves are owned by state-owned or national oil companies (NOCs). Therein lays the challenge. IOCs must work with NOCs to drill and extract hydrocarbons where sovereign nations own the mineral rights. Several Middle East NOCs are susceptible to geopolitical risk where oil or gas production may be potentially at risk. In 2011, Middle East turmoil in Libya and Egypt are excellent cases of production disruption and increased geopolitical risk. In Chapter 13, Bidding and Production Rights, we will review some the various oil and gas regulatory structures that exist.

In the oil and gas industry, reserves are often thought of as one of the key metrics. It is, in one regard, the end game. As previously mentioned, integrated majors have the traditional upstream (exploration and production) and downstream (refining and retailing) business model. Depending on the company, there also may be a midstream sector that includes pipeline, transportation, or storage operations. Midstream typically refers to business operations of refined fuels transport and storage. Within the industry, there are companies that are exclusively dedicated to the midstream segment of oil and gas operations.

Reserve growth is increasingly elusive. IOCs seek to work with NOCs, often in geographically challenging areas. Exploration for hydrocarbons is taking place in the deep waters of the South Atlantic and the frigid waters of Greenland and the Arctic Circle. In addition, IOCs are working with NOCs in geopolitically challenging areas around the world. One can easily imagine the challenges associated with working in Nigeria, Iraq, Venezuela, and the South China Sea.

In Chapter 2, we will explore the investment opportunities and challenges associated with countries such as Iraq, Australia, and Brazil. Each of these three countries presents a significant unique opportunity and set of challenges. Drilling opportunities in all three countries are highly sought after by the industry with companies from around the globe participating in the numerous oil and gas concessions that have been established.

Regulatory Environment

Spurred by the disastrous BP oil spill, many countries implemented deepwater drilling regulatory reviews. The explosion resulted in a six-month oil drilling moratorium in the U.S. portion of the Gulf of Mexico and lasting implications for the industry. What will be the ultimate effects?

Regulation has become one of the single biggest risks to the oil and gas industry. Certainly the U.S. oilfield service sector was adversely impacted as (according to U.S. government estimates) 35 drill rigs and thousands of workers were idled in the U.S. Gulf of Mexico. A small number of drill rigs left the Gulf of Mexico for the west coast of Africa and the South Atlantic. While many drill rig operators chose to stay and wait out the moratorium, the ensuing regulatory changes require producers to disclose their emergency response initiatives and safety plans. These are all very necessary, even critical, to both regulators and investors alike who need to assess possible risks.

Countries all over the globe are reevaluating drilling safety procedures and drilling operations. In addition, Australia and many European countries including

Norway began initiatives aimed at reviewing new licenses for deepwater drilling. Norway, however, recently announced that it did not see any reason to impose a moratorium on deepwater drilling.

While many countries share in the concern for deepwater accidents, there are still others that are encouraging deepwater drilling. In addition, many of these countries see deepwater drilling as an economic opportunity and are not willing to unnecessarily curtail deepwater drilling. Brazil is a case in point, where deepwater drilling represents a significant economic boon to its oil and gas infrastructure and has become a decade-long initiative. Part of the Brazilian plan includes growth in its domestic drill rig and related oilfield service sector infrastructure.

Alternative Energy Forms

Alternative energy, in all of its forms, has a bright future. However, many energy analysts, including myself, conclude that the growth in alternative energy will not achieve the scale necessary to significantly reduce reliance on hydrocarbon-based fossil fuels. That said, alternative energy will play an important role in the future global energy matrix and offers investors significant opportunities over the next decade.

This book will explore advances and investment opportunities in wind, solar, nuclear, geothermal, and hydro power. We will also examine new advances in clean coal technology, biofuels, and the rise and fall of the carbon-trading arena. The birth of the carbon-trading arena partially resulted from efforts to reduce emissions among power producers and other major users of fossil fuels and to transfer wealth from developed countries to less industrial countries.

In the near future, progress will be made in solar photovoltaic panels and wind turbine technologies. Currently, solar photovoltaic panels are enjoying resurgence in markets around the globe. Developments of wind farms are slowing as prices for natural gas soften and power generators seek lower-cost alternatives. Both solar photovoltaic panels and wind power projects are susceptible to the loss of government incentives as many nations can no longer afford to sustain subsidies. This book shall assess markets for natural gas, solar energy, and wind farms to uncover opportunities and challenges associated with all energy forms.

Alternative Energy Growth

Green investing has taken on a new level of importance in today's energy matrix. Companies, both large and small, are developing technologies to better utilize natural resources. Some of the most appealing and early investment opportunities

TABLE 1.1   2010 Primary Fuel Source by Region (tonnes of oil equivalent)

Region	Oil	Natural Gas	Coal	Nuclear	Hydro	Total
North America	1025.5	736.6	531.3	212.7	158.3	2664.4
South & Central America	256.0	121.2	22.5	4.7	158.4	562.8
Europe/Eurasia	913.9	952.8	456.4	265.0	182.0	2770.1
Middle East	336.3	311.0	9.2	0	2.4	658.9
Africa	144.2	84.6	107.3	2.7	22.0	360.8
Asia Pacific	1206.2	446.9	2151.6	125.3	217.1	4147.1

Source: BP Statistical Review of World Energy June 2010.

lay with manufacturers of wind turbines and solar photovoltaic panels. In Chapters 18 and 19, we will examine the successes, challenges, and issues surrounding both wind and solar power.

In addition, in Chapters 16 and 17, we will explore new inroads and thinking into today's hydro power and nuclear energy. Nuclear energy, while still decreasing in use around the globe, is coming under increased scrutiny in the wake of the Japan nuclear disaster. Germany recently took steps to reassess use of nuclear energy while other alternative forms gain traction and scale as shown in Table 1.1. However, many countries are still discouraging its use.

Solar Energy

Use of solar photovoltaic cells to produce electricity is growing throughout North America and Europe driven by governmental incentives. Such incentives have been designed to encourage investment and development of solar energy initiatives. Many project organizers are quickly working to secure investment before governments begin to curtail subsidies for solar energy projects.

One of the bigger challenges associated with solar energy is its limited application—it is confined to regions with plentiful sunlight. In addition, lack of storage may be challenging for solar photovoltaic power generators. Concentrated solar-power generation does have storage capabilities, which we will discuss in Chapter 19. Solar is a useful supplemental power source to augment primary grid sources during peak-use hours.

Currently, Germany is making significant inroads into solar photovoltaic cell investments. The challenge in Germany and other countries becomes the relative cheapness of natural gas compared to using solar energy. The relative decline of natural gas costs compared to other energy forms has become a bit of a conundrum in the industry. Nevertheless, solar photovoltaic cell technology is growing and we'll look at opportunities in this venue.

Wind Power

In recent years, wind power has witnessed growth amid the increase in governmental subsidies made available to power generators. Wind farms were beginning to expand in countries like Spain and Germany, but recently are facing increased challenges with the end of subsidies. The advent of the economic slowdown in OECD countries has meant a decrease in governmental subsidies for wind farms. Many generators were relying on these subsidies and today find themselves in a cost structure pinch.

Wind, as an energy form, is not the least expensive energy form. As an energy form, wind power is still more expensive than natural gas on a per-kilowatt-hour basis. However, there should be continued demand for wind farms throughout OECD countries.

Wind farms are also under similar economic pressures that are befalling solar projects. Natural gas has become so inexpensive and U.S. supplies so plentiful that many generators are waiting for the economics to improve before further investing in wind farms. Wind farms are expected to see improved economics over the mid to longer term.

Nuclear Energy

Nuclear energy remains an enigma in the energy industry. After the Three Mile Island nuclear accident in central Pennsylvania, growth of nuclear energy as an energy form was virtually halted. Today, we know that nuclear energy for all of its ills is still very cost effective and one of the least expensive energy forms.

However, building a new nuclear power plant is very costly and taking place virtually nowhere in the world. The United States and France are the biggest users of the energy form. Both countries have decreased use of nuclear-generated electricity in 2009 versus 2008, likely due to the global economic downturn. Russia and Japan have increased usage of electricity generated by nuclear power during this same period. Unlike many OECD members, Russia's economy has been growing in recent years. Japan's increase in nuclear usage indicates that its commercial and industrial sector was in a modest growth mode prior to the March 2011 earthquake. Chapter 17 will address new advances that have been made to improve safety in nuclear energy and examine the economics of nuclear energy and its cost effectiveness.

Coal Energy

While coal supplies are in relative abundance, the coal industry is under tremendous pressure to develop and institutionalize clean-coal technologies. In order to reduce carbon emissions, OECD countries are aggressively taking steps to reduce usage of coal. The United States still remains a significant coal user. Coal usage is decreasing in the U.S. market, albeit in small increments.

However, non-OECD countries such as China and Russia are continuing to utilize coal as a significant part of their energy matrix. Australia is another significant user of coal, but is actively taking steps to decrease usage. Many of the challenges surrounding coal in countries such as China and India are due to lack of existing infrastructure to transport and store the cleaner fuel natural gas. Eventually, that will change and natural gas will become an appealing alternative energy form. Such changes may be a decade away as infrastructure is built.

In the meantime, profitability for coal producers in North America and Europe is beginning to drop as usage decreases. North American and European coal producers are the first to bear the brunt of a shift away from coal to cleaner-burning fuels. The environmental benefits are expected to be considerable as coal-generating emissions decrease.

Hydro Energy

Hydro energy is experiencing resurgence as generators increasingly build environmentally friendlier structures than in prior years. According to the *BP Statistical Review of World Energy June 2010*, China, Brazil, and Canada are the biggest users of hydro power today. Hydro power does not work in every country or region. Like nuclear, the costs of building a hydro plant are exorbitant. Partnerships and joint ventures are a fiscal necessity. Municipalities and regulators are increasingly open to hydro power plants when the environmental footprint is smaller and steps taken to lessen the overall environmental impact.

Alternative Energy Incentives

Alternative energy has been given a boost by recent tax incentives in the United States and other OECD countries aimed at increasing investment in alternative forms of energy. Like its hydrocarbon brethren, alternative energies are subject to changing regulation around the globe. Nuclear power continues to be highly regulated for all of the obvious reasons. Since the Three Mile Island incident, appetite for nuclear energy has been lackluster at best. Other notable incidents include the nuclear accident at the Chernobyl Nuclear Power Plant in Ukraine on April 26, 1986 and the failure of four reactors at Japan's Tokyo Electric Power Company in March 2011. Since then, nuclear energy has seen better days. However, 25 years later, nuclear technology has improved despite continuing risks.

While incentives for alternative energy forms have proliferated in the United States and Europe, they are quickly going away. We caution investors to review the subsidy structure for power generators in wind and solar power in particular. The global economic slowdown has resulted in governments curtailing subsidies. This may be temporary, but prepare for a more enduring environment with less governmental support for power generators. Many generators are already in a very vulnerable position, particularly in Spain where subsidies have already been cut as a consequence of governmental belt tightening.

Energy Investment Cost Considerations

The costs associated with building a nuclear power plant or hydro project have escalated. Today, there is virtually no energy company that would contemplate building or pursuing a major infrastructure project on its own. Consortiums are the order of the day and will continue to be over the long term. While large energy companies tend to have access to the capital markets and considerable financial resources, partnering has become an economic and, to some extent, financial and operational necessity for large-scale infrastructure energy projects.

Refinery upgrading, pipeline building, or alternative energy projects require such considerable financial resources that multiple companies will partner to manage risk and share costs. An example of such a project is the Petrobras's Abreu y Lima refinery in the Brazilian state of Pernambuco in collaboration with Petróleos de Venezuela, S.A. This project has been on the drawing board for years with the projected cost increasing each passing year. Current total project cost estimates are in the US$11 billion range. Would a major energy company contemplate such a project on a stand-alone basis? It's not likely.

Each project is evaluated on a return on investment, return on capital employed, and debt repayment basis by the project owners and investors. Their investment criteria are complex and unique to their own time horizon, due diligence, and risk appetite. We will look at a few project opportunities as examples of how investors may participate.

Concluding Thoughts

Energy is indeed a strategic and economic imperative that warrants the savviest investor's time and attention. Whether stocks, fixed income opportunities, exchange traded funds, or commodity-based funds, energy holds investment promise. In the chapters that follow, we hope to illustrate some of the varied opportunities and provide a basis for further due diligence by both investors and others who have an interest in this complex industry.

This is a technology intensive industry, which only reinforces the importance of private sector investment, and progress is indeed being made. For example, carbon capture and storage holds promise as coal producers have found ways to produce what we refer to as a *cleaner coal*. The carbon capture and storage process can extract contaminants from coal while helping to revitalize mature oil wells. We will review cleaner coal developments in later chapters.

We will also review renewable energy, nuclear energy, geothermal, and hydro forms of electricity production and their potential growth opportunities. There have been considerable technological advances in the nuclear, wind, and solar arenas. An exciting development is that of solar power generation which can now store heat energy for later use. Technological enhancements are taking this industry to places once thought unimaginable. While there have been advances in nuclear technology, we believe that its use as a power source will be set back on the heels of Japan's March 2011 nuclear accident at the Tokyo Electric Power Company's nuclear plant.

CHAPTER 2

Investment Opportunities in Energy

In this chapter, we review some of the more promising investment opportunities in the energy industry. Several opportunities are identified below. This list is not all inclusive. The opportunities on the short list are the developments in Australian natural gas and Brazil's deepwater crude oil basins. Other opportunities that warrant consideration are developments in Iraq. While Iraq is still very much in transition, many private companies have already seized the moment and ventured into this market, expecting future growth. While still wrought with risk, Iraq's political situation has not deterred many of the integrated majors. Finally, we assess alternative energy and some of the developments in this arena.

Asia Comes of Age

The global financial crisis of 2008 to 2009 aptly illustrated the resilience of the Chinese economy through its government's massive stimulus spending equivalent to US$586 billion designed to jumpstart its economy and any other economy supported by the Chinese economy. Today, there isn't a major industry not impacted by China's seemingly insatiable consumption of commodities, autos, and energy.

China has become a force to be reckoned with in energy circles. China's demand for crude and crude-related products will buoy both near- and midterm crude oil demand. This translates into healthy crude oil demand coming out of one of the most robust global economies. This also means that the Chinese industrial sector is rapidly expanding production capabilities and securing future sources of energy. China has been aggressively courting some very large energy producers such as Petróleos de Venezuela, S.A. (PDVSA), Russia's

Gazprom, and other Middle Eastern and Asian energy producers. What has become apparent is Chinese necessity to secure future energy sources to meet its domestic demand.

Australia's Natural Gas Boom

Australia is going through a natural gas renaissance as numerous fields holding what is called *tight gas* are being developed. From an investment perspective, this is appealing for several reasons, including the fact that Australia is an excellent place in which to do business. Overall, Australia is a low risk environment with a business-friendly energy regulatory framework. These tight gas fields are predominantly located in Western Australia, New South Wales, and Queensland. Numerous global companies have already established a presence, and more are vying for acreage. According to the *BP Statistical Review of World Energy June 2010*, Australia's proven natural gas reserves are 108.7 trillion cubic feet (3.08 trillion cubic meters).

Because Australia is so distant from any other market, the production from natural gas fields that have been developed is converted to liquefied natural gas (LNG) and primarily transported to Asian markets. Most of the LNG is exported by ship to Japan, South Korea, China, and Indonesia. Certainly, pipeline structures are not practical or economical. This is a great example of an opportunity to participate in growing Asian emerging markets.

Natural gas will have a promising future. Because it is considered a clean fuel, and can be converted to LNG, the possibilities grow significantly. What does that mean? Of all fossil fuel energy sources, natural gas emits the least emissions into the atmosphere. Consequently, I believe the longer-term demand for natural gas and LNG is going nowhere but up.

Asian demand for natural gas does not appear to be slowing. Other regional markets include India, Malaysia, and neighboring New Zealand. Projected 2011 GDP is in the 8 percent to 9 percent range for both China and India. Long-term contracts have been set up between project producers and those Asian purchasers of LNG with growing demand.

One of the largest natural gas fields is the Western Australian Gorgon project with a concession consisting of the Australian subsidiaries of Chevron, ExxonMobil, and Shell. Chevron Australia is the operator, with a 50 percent interest. ExxonMobil's and Shell's Australian subsidiaries each have a 25 percent interest. The Gorgon LNG project is one of the largest LNG projects in the energy markets today. According to a September 19, 2009, Chevron press release, the Gorgon project has reserve potential of 40 trillion cubic feet and an economic life of 40 years from the time of startup. First gas is estimated for 2014. In addition, according to Chevron's statement, the Gorgon project production levels are equivalent to 6.7 billion barrels of oil. One can refer to Chevron (www. Chevron.com) for more information on this promising project.

Other Australian LNG projects include that of UK-based BG Group Plc. According to a November 1, 2010, press release, the BG Group's US$15 billion investment in Australia's Queensland primarily targets Asian users of LNG. The release states contracts to convert coal-seam gas to LNG are already established with customers in China, Japan, Singapore, and Chile. The BG group states the project will have a 20-year operating life.

LNG should have a very good long-term investment proposition as countries with growing energy needs seek this clean fuel alternative. As long as a country is not land-locked, there is opportunity to build infrastructure to receive LNG shipments.

Brazil Beckons with Deepwater

Brazil is in a unique position in the global energy industry. Not only has Brazil evolved into an economic powerhouse, but an energy powerhouse as well. Brazil has garnered a place at the table with the world's integrated majors and its state-owned oil company Petróleos Brasileiros S.A. (known as Petrobras) is here to stay. Over the last decade, Petrobras has quietly been investing in deepwater technology, research, and improving its upstream capabilities. In 2006, the deepwater discoveries of the Lula field (formerly the Tupi field) in the South Atlantic propelled Petrobras onto the global energy stage. Oil and gas companies make discoveries with some level of frequency. Why the added attention? Petrobras discovered one of the largest oil and gas fields in the Americas since the Cantarell discovery in the 1970s in the Gulf of Mexico by Petróleos Mexicanos (PEMEX).

Petrobras is no stranger to deepwater drilling. In the ensuing years, much research went into understanding the geology and finding hydrocarbons under a layer of salt thousands of meters under the sea floor. These reserves are known as pre-salt reserves. Since then, Petrobras has made other discoveries in neighboring fields such as Franco, Libra, and several others. What has become evident is the prevalence of similar geology in the areas off the coast of Rio de Janeiro. The basins of Santos and Campos hold what could be very significant reserves. Please refer to Figure 2.1, which illustrates all three of Brazil's offshore crude and natural gas basins. And, as such, the basins off the Brazilian coast make my short list of global opportunities to have on our radar.

Even though Petrobras is a national oil company, it warrants any savvy investor's attention. Much has been made of its recent capitalization, which we'll come back to in Chapter 4, however, despite the fact that the Brazilian government has increased its ownership in Petrobras, investing here is definitely an attractive longer-term proposition.

FIGURE 2.1   Brazil Basins

Reserves Are the Story

In an era where new hydrocarbon reserves are increasingly found in the globe's most challenging places, the deep waters of the South Atlantic are of interest. Prior to the pre-salt discoveries, Petrobras had proven hydrocarbon reserves of approximately 12 billion barrels of oil equivalent (BOE) based on U.S. Securities and Exchange Commission (SEC) criteria and approximately 14.8 billion in reserves under Society of Petroleum Engineers (SPE) criteria. There will be more on the SEC and SPE criteria in Chapter 6. Overall, 12 billion BOE is by itself not too much to get excited about. The pre-salt discoveries in the Lula and other adjacent fields, added another 2 billion BOE (under SPE criteria) to Petrobras' proven reserve base.

Based on their geological analyses, the Brazilian regulator Agencia Nacional do Petróleos (ANP) estimates reserve potential upward of 30 billion BOE in the larger Santos Basin. On October 29, 2010, the ANP announced that the Libra field may hold up to 15 billion barrels of recoverable oil, potentially surpassing that of the Lula field. This estimate is subject to the certification process of industry experts. These estimates are garnering substantial attention in energy circles around the globe.

As such, global oil and gas producers are rushing to the South Atlantic to establish a presence and obtain acreage. According to the ANP, there are now approximately 75 concessions operating in the Campos and Santos basins.

In 2009, the Brazilian government announced that all offshore fields were now designated "Key Strategic Areas," and as such would no longer be included in future bid rounds. More importantly, the government overhauled the energy framework by designating Petrobras the "operator," with a 30 percent interest in all key strategic areas. Operators under the prior concession framework were grandfathered in and their contracts honored. New concessions would be subject to the new energy policy with Petrobras as operator. Onshore concessions would continue to operate under the prior concession framework.

The question becomes, why the changes? It's simple. Reserve potential is one of the end games in the industry and the Brazilian government moved to preserve Petrobras's position and secure future energy sources for the country's growing domestic economy. Would an independent oil and gas company leave reserves "on the table" or beneath the ocean floor? Such a strategy would be unthinkable. Most investors are not at all surprised at Petrobras's desire to develop these fields.

Considerable costs are involved to develop these basins and I anticipate that Petrobras may go back to the drawing board and revisit its existing capital expenditure (capex) plan equivalent to US$224 billion to be invested from 2010 to 2014. Given the geology and enormity of the area, it is conceivable that its capex plan will grow over the near to mid term. Invariably, Petrobras will have to tap debt markets to pursue this massive project. In addition, given the scale of the project, Petrobras could become a serial bond issuer. There will be more on this later in Chapter 4.

What does this mean for investors? It is within the realm of possibility that Petrobras, in order to develop these fields, will be forced to incur additional levels of debt over the mid- to long-term time horizon. For Petrobras, it's the cost of doing business. My own assessment is that as long as Petrobras remains investment grade, I would keep it in your portfolio. Currently, Petrobras is investment grade by all the major rating agencies. Remember, nothing here is short term in nature. Few other global energy companies have plans to almost double production. Over the mid-term, I believe Petrobras and the South Atlantic will be a good investment opportunity.

Why keep it in a portfolio? It's simple, there are few, if any, majors that have a plan in place to double hydrocarbon production and potentially double the reserve base over the next decade. If Saudi Aramco was developing these fields, investors would be lining up to participate. Think very long term. Near term,

Petrobras' stock price may falter and earnings per share could come up short. It doesn't matter. No other integrated major is sitting on the geological fields to which Petrobras can lay claim. Geology matters in this industry.

There was much discussion as to whether majors would retain interest in Brazil under this new regulatory framework. I believe there is plenty of global interest in these fields, provided government regulation doesn't change from its current state and become overly intrusive. For investors, I believe the South Atlantic warrants attention. There are many companies participating in these concessions, BG Group, Repsol, Shell, Chevron, and ExxonMobil to name just a few. Again, production from these blocks will evolve over the next decade. The pre-salt layers are definitely an area to keep watching.

Iraq's Road to Recovery

After years of neglect, sanctions, and underinvestment, Iraq's energy sector has come a long way. While there is much work ahead, Iraq has revitalized its oil and gas sector under Oil Minister Hussain al-Shahristani. Iraq has implemented its first two bid rounds that attracted the participation by most of the largest oil majors. Given the complexities and challenges associated with Iraq, why is it on my short list of investment opportunities? In the Middle East, a region that has very limited opportunity for investors, Iraq is one of the few investment opportunities available. There are numerous global oil and gas companies that have ventured into this arena with the hopes of establishing a foothold in what I would refer to as a frontier in the oil industry.

Iraq is indeed a frontier and a diamond in the rough. It doesn't take much to appreciate the fact that Iraq is sitting on some of the world's largest oil reserves. Iraq's oil ministry just revised its proven reserves to 143 billion (BOE) from 113 billion BOE. Iraq ranks in the top five in terms of oil reserves, placing its proven reserves on par with Iran, Kuwait, and other Middle Eastern countries. In Chapter 6, we'll discuss reserves and its criteria.

Iraq is going to need considerable investment infrastructure to meet the needs of future oil and gas production growth. According to the U.S. Energy Information Administration (EIA), Iraq's 2009 crude oil production was 2.4 million barrels per day (mmbpd). Iraq's pre-war crude oil production capacity was 2.8 mmbpd. Iraq currently is seeking investment of approximately US$20 billion to build additional refining capacity over the next decade. Much of its existing refining infrastructure is in dire need of repair and has not been upgraded in decades. As a result, Iraq's refining utilization rate is in the 60 to 75 percent range, according to the EIA.

This is a situation that will play out over the next two decades. What is uncertain is the government's role, policy, regulation, and energy framework. To date, Iraq has instituted western-style bid rounds to secure investment in several large oil fields.

While Iraq's bid rounds did get off to a bumpy start, Iraq is slowly gaining ground in establishing itself at the Organization of the Petroleum Exporting Countries (OPEC) table. Unlike its OPEC counterparts, Iraq is currently exempt from OPEC production quotas.

Reserves Are the Big Story in Iraq

In October 2010, Mr. al Shahristani announced an increase in Iraqi proven oil reserves to 143 billion BOE from 113 billion BOE. This is important for a number of reasons. First, it illustrates that Iraq is actively getting its reserves certified by the select group of authorities in the industry that carry out the certification process. There are some that doubt Iraq's reserve estimation. I think there would be far more damage to Iraq's standing in the industry with an inaccurate estimate. Generally, proven reserve estimates are provided in the independent reserve certification process.

Iraq's West Qurna oil field represents one of the largest on the planet with almost 143 billion BOE in reserves. To put this in perspective, the industry is rushing to the South Atlantic to work in Brazil for potentially 8 to 15 billion BOE. West Qurna represents significant opportunity for development over the next two decades. Table 2.1 illustrates Iraq's reserves and production by Iraqi national oil companies. The reserve total of 113 billion barrels does not reflect the newly released reserve estimate.

According to the Iraq Oil Ministry, 71 percent of Iraq's oil reserves are in the south, 20 percent in the north, and the remainder in the center of the country. According to the EIA, Iraq's Ministry of Oil controls oil and gas production in

TABLE 2.1   Iraq 2010 Reserves and Production

Iraq Oil Co.	No. of Fields	Reserves (BN of Barrels)	2010 Production (Thousand bpd)	Potential Production (Thousand bpd)
KRG	6	2	15	375
North Oil Co.	32	21	770	1,300
Midland Oil Co.	27	13	10	680
Missan Oil Co.	10	8	110	820
South Oil Co.	25	69	1,455	10,050
Total	100	113	2,360	13,225

Source: Iraq Oil Ministry.

all but the Kurdish-governed parts of the country. These regions are operated by Kurdish Regional Government (KRG). Table 2.1 illustrates that the North Oil Company and the South Oil Company, collectively, operate 94 percent of Iraq's annual production and 80 percent of its proven reserves. The vast majority of Iraq reserve potential is also situated in the strategic North and South regions of the country.

Refining Infrastructure

Iraq currently has 11 refineries with approximately 700,000 barrels per day (bpd) in refining capacity. After years of neglect, underinvestment, and war, Iraq's infrastructure is in dire need of improvement. The Iraqi Oil Ministry is currently seeking private-sector investment to build and operate four new refineries to process Iraq's growing crude production. Currently, Iraq's refineries are operating at a utilization rate of approximately 60 to 75 percent. According to the EIA, Iraq is seeking approximately $20 billion in refining investments among two or three engineering and construction firms currently indentified to participate in these infrastructure projects to add 740,000 bpd in new refining capacity.

The Oil Ministry requires 75 percent of employees to be Iraqi citizens and prohibits private ownership of land. Crude purchases are to be market-based with pricing based on Dated Brent with various economic, pricing, and tax incentives. The projects require building pipeline infrastructure to deliver crudes to the new refineries. The infrastructure projects can easily take the better part of the next decade. This is a potential opportunity for a joint venture or consortium to partner in developing a refinery. Infrastructure projects of this magnitude will undoubtedly have continuous oversight by various Iraqi authorities.

Risks Abound

The biggest risks are political risks, security risks, and risks of the unknown a decade down the road. Will the government, and future governments, be able to withstand corruption, instability, and the numerous political factions that add to Iraq's complex landscape? Will Iraq's current fragile government cave to insurgents and retrench or move forward with infrastructure projects and investment from the global energy community? It is impossible to know the future political risks. To date, there are strong efforts being made to secure long-term contracts, invite investment, and proceed with the development of several major oil and gas fields.

This is a situation of investing with eyes wide open. There are several companies that are participating in various fields and projects that I believe hold promise. Shell, Total, BP, and ExxonMobil have secured an interest in Iraq's first two bid rounds and various projects. These institutions have the financial wherewithal and long-term investment patience to invest in a complex and uncertain market like Iraq. Be mindful that these projects are structured as service contracts prohibiting international oil companies from increasing reserves or adding to their crude oil production base. Again, Iraq is a long-term investment story and as such, companies such as Shell and Total will see the fruits of these efforts over the next decade. Work that is being done today is laying the groundwork for continued access to a region previously off limits to western companies.

North American Unconventional Natural Gas Plays

In recent years, one of the most significant opportunities to arise is the emergence of unconventional natural gas shale plays. The United States and Canada are home to vast resources of unconventional natural gas virtually ensuring natural gas supplies to North America for potentially the next two decades.

The challenges are considerable as the natural gas industry grapples with both the technology used to commercialize these reserves and the economic cost at which these reserves can be extracted. Neither of these challenges can be considered separately. At U.S. natural gas prices of less than $4.50 per mmBtu, development of unconventional natural gas shale plays will remain stagnant. At approximately $7.00 mmBtu, development becomes more economical for producers. Meanwhile, the race by global producers to acquire U.S. acreage has begun.

What Are Unconventional Natural Gas Shales?

Unconventional natural gas shales are pockets of natural gas tightly locked in layers of sedimentary shale rock. In the U.S. and Canadian markets, there is growing interest in the large basins of unconventional natural gas shale in the Marcellus, Haynesville, Barnett, Bakken, Eagle Ford, and other fields. The deposits hold great promise for additional natural gas supply for both the U.S. and Canadian domestic markets.

The Issues

At issue is whether the process used for extracting these reserves has the potential to contaminate the water table. Many energy industry research groups are conducting independent research to determine whether there is any possibility of contamination. The U.S. Environmental Protection Agency (EPA) is also conducting its research to determine any potential impact on the water table. As of the writing, there hasn't been any definitive direction from the EPA.

Technology

The technology used for extracting unconventional natural gas generally utilizes water, drilling fluids, and sand at high pressures (from 80 pounds per square inch (psi) and higher, with some applications approaching 15,000 psi) to break layers of sedimentary rock. This process is known as hydraulic fracturing and the subject of much debate. The concern centers around the drilling fluids used to break apart the sedimentary rocks and the possibility that they could contaminate the water table. The State of New York has banned this process to protect New York City's water table. Pennsylvania may take steps to curtail additional leases and permits. As of yet, it is important to note that potential hazards have not yet been substantiated.

I am enthused about this market, as many global producers are already rushing to acquire acreage in the United States. There are indeed foreign producers such as Reliance (India), Total (France), and Chinese energy companies that have already acquired acreage with various joint venture partners in the U.S. market. Natural gas is a cleaner fuel than other fossil fuel forms and has the potential to meet decades of energy demand in the North American economies.

Solar Power Generation

Solar photovoltaic panels and wind energy have the potential to augment peak electricity demand in select markets. While there are several investment opportunities around the world, it is essential to thoroughly analyze the cost structure, which varies widely by project and country. Renewable energy infrastructure projects come with steep price tags. However, many governments are offering economic incentives to electricity project sponsors.

One of the more promising areas of renewable energy is that of solar power generation which utilizes parabolic mirrors to heat fluids and store heat energy for later use. The process of heating fluids enables power producers to produce electricity at night or when there is no sunshine. Because of its storage capabilities, we anticipate this technology will have wider appeal.

Concluding Thoughts

Opportunities in the energy industry are considerable. The complex landscape necessitates due diligence and understanding of both the opportunities and challenges in natural gas, LNG, and shale formations. In traditional energy investments, we look to Brazil, North American natural gas shales, and Iraq. All have certain levels of risk. However, these areas are the growth areas in the industry.

In alternative energy, look to solar power generation for future growth potential. In Chapter 19, we describe differences in solar power generation. There are technological differences that make certain projects potentially more appealing. Investors interested in renewable energy will find opportunities in wind power, hydro, and geothermal, which will be reviewed in Parts III and IV of the book. Among my favorites is that of concentrating solar power generation, because of its storage capabilities.

CHAPTER 3

Cash Flow and Liquidity at Various Crude Prices

Cash flow remains the holy grail of all energy companies and the yardstick by which these companies are measured in terms of their ability to meet capital expenditure plans and growth targets. We first review its impact on capital spending and evaluative criteria common to all oil companies including both independent oil companies (IOCs) and national oil companies (NOCs). We also review the importance of liquidity, cash flow, and leverage on the impact on capital expenditure planning.

Independent Oil Companies

Among oil and gas producers, cash flow is directly affected by crude oil prices. In recent years, we have witnessed extremes at both ends of the crude price spectrum. In 2007 and 2008, crude prices continued their ascent into the $80 to $100 per barrel price range. By July 2008, crude oil prices reached a record high of $147.11 per barrel, heralding a vibrant third quarter earnings season only to be marred by the momentous collapse of both Lehman Brothers and AIG in September 2008. By December 2008, crude oil prices dropped to near $30 per barrel.

The industry has not witnessed such extremes in prices in recent memory. How do producers react and manage budgets, strategy planning, and capital expenditures in such price extremes? How do NOCs react to price swings? Are they as Flexible and agile as their IOC counterparts?

A high crude oil price enables IOCs to invest in higher cost, lower margin, lower return projects that might not otherwise meet economic hurdles. In general, IOCs enjoy a level of financial flexibility not permitted by NOCs. If, for example, a given project is profitable at $50 per barrel, but not at $30 per barrel, there is a direct impact on the profitability of these producers. All producers, IOCs and NOCs alike, will review projects based on a given breakeven in terms of a minimum hurdle crude oil price.

During extreme price volatility, IOCs are considerably better at managing and preserving adequate levels of liquidity. IOCs implement institution-wide cost management programs aimed at cutting costs virtually across the board. Most IOCs will leave exploration and production (E&P) budget cutting as a last resort. If a project doesn't meet break even or cost hurdles, it gets placed on the back burner until crude oil prices increase to justify proceeding. An example might include certain Canadian oil sand projects that require a higher crude oil price in order to preserve the economics and make it a viable project. These Canadian crudes require upgrading and are a heavier, sour grade of crude. Certain Canadian oil projects require a $40 per barrel or higher oil price to make it economically appealing to IOCs.

In a low crude oil-price environment, it is common for capital expenditure budgets to come under review, and perhaps get decreased as management focuses its efforts on the higher margin projects. While exploration and production are the last to be affected, every project has a breakeven and its own set of project hurdles.

National Oil Companies

As one might expect, NOCs do not have the financial flexibility of IOCs. NOCs are not nearly as agile as IOCs for a plethora of reasons. In a low crude oil-price environment, NOCs' economic contributions to their home countries are dramatically reduced. As such, painful decisions often have to be made. In most cases, revenue from NOCs directly funds domestic education, healthcare, and a wide variety of other non-energy essentials.

In a low crude oil-price environment, the tables often get turned whereby NOCs need the investment capabilities of IOCs as joint venture partners. NOCs simply need the investment capital to pursue marginal projects. In many cases, like at IOCs, lower margin projects get shelved until crude prices rebound and the economics improve.

Additional complexities include potential currency price devaluation and possible inflation, both of which can compound the adverse effect of low crude oil prices. This was evident in NOCs in Russia, Venezuela, and Mexico as crude prices declined to 10-year lows of $30 per barrel in December 2008. Both the Mexican Peso and Venezuelan Bolivar suffered devaluations concurrent with the collapse of crude prices. In both cases, revenues declined resulting in negative net margins and significant decreases in cash flow. Budgetary cuts and capital expenditure decreases were necessary.

NOCs are not often able to compensate for decreases in crude oil prices elsewhere in the home government's budgets. For NOCs, oil and gas-based royalties could contribute up to 50 percent of government revenues. Tax increases are often frowned upon by politicians. While economically necessary, tax increases also upset the electorate which does play a role in national policy for NOCs.

Capital Expenditure Planning

Capital expenditure planning differs from large-cap integrated majors such as many IOCs to small-cap oil juniors. The key is to have a portfolio of producing assets within a variety of life cycles. In other words, it is critical to oil and gas producers to have early-stage assets with future growth potential as well as more mature assets that are at or near peak production. In addition, many of the integrated majors and other large independents will have assets that are in the pure research stage of development. This is a costly endeavor not often undertaken by micro-cap or small-cap firms.

Exploration and Production Portfolio

Portfolio management is critical for oil and gas producers, particularly during the commodity downturn. Each producer must continually assess the maturity of their portfolio. In other words, every producer should have newer assets early in their production life cycle. Producers should have assets that are at or are near their peak production cycle. These assets are near their peak production capability, producing large amounts of cash flow. Finally, there will be older, more mature assets that are in the twilight of their production.

Newer assets have the greatest future cash flow potential. At the same time, these assets have the greatest and most immediate infrastructure and capital expenditure demands. It may take four to eight years before these assets become cash-flow positive. These assets require considerable investment in their early years.

Downturns in the commodity cycle have a more dramatic impact on small-cap firms such oil juniors. Many of these firms will curtail drilling and development activities until crude oil prices bounce back. Margins come under extreme pressure and many small- and micro-cap firms will find themselves in a negative cash flow situation. Access to cash and liquidity measures are of critical importance to these firms.

Downstream Divestitures

Downstream oil operations continue to come under pressure for both IOCs and NOCs. As we might expect, budgets will contract as investment moves to the more profitable upstream operations. Increasingly razor-thin margins in downstream operations have resulted in many divestitures of retail assets.

Around the globe, both IOCs and NOCs are increasingly divesting their large retail operations. This phenomenon is taking place in the United States, Europe, and Latin America. No longer are large oil companies retaining the traditional gas station and convenience store model. Today, both NOCs and IOCs are leasing their names and selling the assets to distributors. Worldwide, the integrated majors are departing the retail sector. The margins in retail gasoline are small, decreasing, and vulnerable to downturns in the commodity cycle. Why risk earnings? The strategy is simply to divest and retain the brand name on the retail assets.

In some cases, regulatory frameworks are behind the sale of retail assets. In many countries, the regulatory environment for retail gasoline stations is highly regulated. As such, earnings for oil and gas companies are continuously at risk in these markets. Argentina is an example of a market that is highly regulated at the local level. It is increasingly challenging for oil and gas producers to have profitable operations. As a result, many producers simply divest operations.

Mexico and Venezuela are other markets that regulate local retail gasoline stations. As a result, NOCs such as PDVSA and PEMEX struggle with downstream earnings. These NOCs don't benefit from increases in gasoline or diesel fuel prices. Many governments simply refuse to raise gasoline or diesel fuel prices at the pump for the electorate.

Refinery Modifications

The global downturn in crude oil demand among Organization for Economic Co-operation and Development (OECD) countries has left the refining sector in the United States and Europe with delayed capital improvements. Today, new refineries in Europe or the United States are unthinkable. There is excess refining capacity. Refinery closures are in vogue as integrated majors in OECD countries continue to battle lackluster crude oil demand. While the global economy is improving, the damage has already been done. As a result of weak crude oil demand, many refineries in North America and Europe were closed.

Emerging market demand is growing. There are new refineries on the drawing board in Brazil, the Middle East, and Asia. These markets are indeed the exception.

In other markets, the more economical strategy is to modify existing refineries instead of building new refineries. Improvements include adding cokers, hydrocrackers, and steam crackers to refine heavier crudes and petrochemicals. Increasingly, refineries seek to purchase higher sulfur, heavy crudes instead of lighter, sweeter crudes. It's more economical to upgrade and process the heavy crude than to purchase and process the more expensive lighter, sweeter crudes.

Modifying refineries is also a costly endeavor. Adding on cokers or hydrocrackers necessitates significant capital expenditure financing. Larger integrated majors can finance these types of projects with greater flexibility than smaller independents.

The strategy is to rationalize refining assets in Europe and the United States. This strategy is going to continue as the global economy emerges from the economic recession of 2008 to 2009. While we are in the midst of a modest recovery, refining demand is still very much lackluster in OECD countries, but considerably stronger in emerging markets.

Liquidity—Cash Is Still King

IOCs often have several back-up lines of credit under pre-arranged bank agreements. In many cases, these back-up lines are unused. During the bull run years where crude prices increased to $147 per barrel, many IOCs utilized the opportunity to build significant cash balances. As one might expect, this strategy paid dividends in many ways. ExxonMobil reported cash balances of near $35 billion at the end of fiscal year 2007. Other IOCs reported impressive cash balances in excess of $5 billion. These war chests enabled many IOCs to weather the economic downturn of early 2009 when crude prices collapsed. Two years later, these companies were ready to strategically deploy these cash balances and take advantage of other opportunities.

From an investment standpoint, continue to focus on a strong balance sheet. Cash and marketable security balances are high on the list of must-haves. Look for unused lines of credit. Most large-cap firms will have ready access to the capital markets. Smaller-cap firms have to have back-up financing plans.

In addition, many large-cap firms employed cost-management strategies in efforts to contain cost structures. These cost-management strategies are instituted at NOCs with similar importance and priority. Each NOC is challenged to manage the budgetary demands of its majority shareholder.

Liquidity comes under extreme pressure with the volatility of the commodity cycle for some NOCs. During the last downturn in commodity prices, some NOCs were adversely affected and experienced decreases in their cash and marketable securities.

Liquidity as a Strategy

For investment purposes, I continue to favor those companies with strong balance sheets with liquidity metrics that are able to withstand the downturn in the commodity cycle. As the commodity cycle improves, those companies that weathered the storm are the ones that will emerge the strongest. This becomes more apparent for companies that have the strongest investment-grade ratings.

A strong balance sheet enables these same institutions to take advantage of opportunities to make acquisitions or participate in joint ventures. These companies are highly sought after as joint venture partners. Liquidity has become a considerable strategic advantage.

Liquidity Metrics

Below are key ratios and metrics to assess liquidity. This is not all inclusive, but will provide a basis from which to form an opinion. There are many other liquidity ratios commonly used. As mentioned before, cash and marketable securities are king. Access to capital is also part of the liquidity equation. A strong balance sheet will go a long way. Three metrics useful in measuring liquidity are:

1. Cash from operations to current liabilities (x)
2. Cash to short-term debt (x)
3. Short-term debt to long-term debt or short term debt to total debt (%)

Cash-Flow Considerations

There is no substitute for cash flow in the energy sector. Whether an energy producer is in renewable energy, nuclear, oil, or gas, the ability to generate sustainable earnings to service debt and carry out its capital expenditure planning is of prime importance. To this end, we favor companies with solid revenue growth and relatively conservative cost structures. The prime importance is sustainable earnings during depressed commodity prices.

The most vulnerable casualty of a downturn in the commodity cycle is cash flow. Cash-flow protection is paramount. The integrated majors or IOCs tend to be very good at instituting cost-management measures. Some NOCs are more challenged in preserving their cash flow.

Cash flow is the basis by which most investment decisions are made. In general, both oil and gas producers will avoid production disruptions to the E&P side of the business. Oil and gas producers will often cut back in other non-production areas before E&P gets impacted.

Project Cost Structures

In a low crude oil-price environment, large-cap producers will often shelve projects that require a higher crude oil price breakeven. Every project has a pre-determined breakeven measured on a per-barrel oil price. Project-level break-even prices vary by project and producer. Every oil and gas producer has a different cost structure. A good example of this is developing Canada's oil sands. This very capital-intensive project may require a crude oil price in excess of $50 per barrel in order to make the economics work. The project breakeven is unique to every firm and based upon its own cost structures.

Another example is the current weakness in the North American natural gas market. Some producers in North America are shelving development of unconventional natural gas shales until natural gas prices improve from below

$4.50/per mmBtu. These producers may require a natural gas price from $6 to $7 per mmBtu.

Cash-Flow Metrics

Cash-flow generation is paramount in the energy sector. We look to revenue growth, earnings generation, and debt service as key factors in assessing the financial health of any company in the energy value chain. Whether a company is an oil producer, natural gas producer, or provides solar energy to a municipality, revenue growth is fundamental to cash-flow growth.

Today, a universal measure of cash flow is the earnings before interest, taxes, depreciation, and amortization (EBITDA) metric often used by bankers, analysts, and others in the financial community. While this is universally understood, there are other metrics that capture the variation in cash flow, such as funds from operations, and other free cash flow measures. As key components to cash flow, we focus on revenue strength and earnings sustainability. Always consider the effects of one-time accounting events such as extraordinary events, asset sales, charge-offs, and the like. It is important to keep in mind that there are numerous variations on these financial metrics widely employed in the financial community. The cash-flow metrics in Table 3.1 are merely one version meant to illustrate the steps taken to obtain free cash flow.

Leverage

Leverage is equally important in assessing the financial health of any company. Concurrent with cash flow and liquidity, a company must be able to service its debt obligations. Downturns in the commodity cycle will place pressure on leverage ratios for both IOCs and NOCs alike. Small-cap firms such as oil juniors are particularly vulnerable as decreases in cash flow can increase leverage ratios.

We favor those companies with conservative balance sheets and those with financial flexibility to withstand economic downturns. Access to capital is always important, as is cash balances.

- EBIT/Interest expense or EBITDA/Interest expense
- Total Debt/EBITDA or Net Debt/EBITDA
- Total Debt/Capital where capital = (total debt + equity)

Table 3.2 illustrates the increase in leverage in 2009 by this sample set of approximately 1,700 energy companies. By 2010, there is modest improvement in credit metrics as companies begin to recover. All told, Net Debt/EBITDA of 1.1x is still relatively strong, all things considered.

TABLE 3.1 Cash Flow Metrics

Ratio	Definition
EBIT + depreciation and amortization	Earnings before interest and taxes*
EBITDA**	Earnings before interest, taxes, depreciation, and amortization expense: a cash-flow measure
− interest paid − taxes paid + dividends received from affiliates	
Funds from Operations +/− changes in working capital	
Cash flow from operations − capital expenditures − dividends	
Free Cash Flow	

Source: Brookshire Advisory and Research, Inc.
*EBIT is essentially operating income or earnings from continuing operations before interest expense and income taxes.
**May include rental expense for a more conservative measure of cash flow, in which case EBITDA becomes EBITDAR

TABLE 3.2 Leverage Ratios 1700 Energy Companies 2006–2010

Ratios	2006	2007	2008	2009	2010
Total Debt/Capital	36.7	35.2	36.3	40.1	38.0
EBITDA/Interest Exp	5.8x	8.3x	10.1x	8.4x	4.0x
Total Debt/EBITDA	1.8x	1.7x	1.9x	2.3x	2.1x
Net Debt/EBITDA	1.1x	0.6x	0.9x	1.2x	1.1x

Source: Copyright © Capital IQ, Inc, a Standard & Poor's business. Standard & Poor's including its subsidiary corporations is a division of The McGraw Hill Companies, Inc. Reproduction of this Chart in any form is prohibited without Capital IQ, Inc.'s prior written permission.

Concluding Thoughts

There is much due diligence that must be completed in the process of evaluating any potential energy investment. Of additional consideration is the role of government loans, guarantees, or other subsidies that often play a role in energy infrastructure projects. Foremost is the ability to generate cash flow amid sustainable earnings and show a growing revenue base.

Cost structures vary widely across the energy value chain. The liquidity, cash flow, and leverage metrics are meant to provide a basic foundation upon which to build in pursuit of additional, deeper analysis. This complex sector has a myriad of factors all critical in understanding an investment opportunity. Whether it is as passive as buying equity or investing in a renewable energy project, the steps are the same. We advocate strong balance sheets, robust revenue growth potential, and sustainable earnings. These factors will provide for continued cash flow to service debt, capital expenditures, and future growth opportunities throughout the commodity cycle.

CHAPTER 4

Capital Structure and Capital Markets

In recent years, maintaining financial flexibility has been the mantra in the energy sector. This chapter reviews some of the market dynamics that energy-sector firms face in the sometimes-tumultuous capital markets. Oil juniors have a different strategy in capital raising than that of integrated majors. We look at both the debt and equity markets and how the capital markets have become somewhat of a life-line for some firms and less so for others. In addition, we review some of the varied investors in the energy sector today. Investors are a demanding group seeking alpha in a variety of investments and transactions. We place the energy sector in a framework by which you can compare differences among financing strategies.

Capital Structure

Capital structure matters a great deal in the investment arena. Energy producers, whether new or established, take steps to enhance and preserve the quality of their capital structure. The quality and strength of an energy producer's capital structure can be a distinct competitive advantage. Producers, whether they are a wind farm or a refinery, must endeavor to find the lowest cost of capital.

In addition, debt and equity markets are not always cooperative. Producers (or issuers) must seize opportunities while the capital markets are available and there is investment appetite for their debt or equity issuances. Costs, pricing, and market timing are significant considerations. Below we review and assess issues in both the debt and equity markets. We then explore who are the investors today in energy.

Debt Markets

The debt markets have been very accessible to investment-grade energy companies, both large and small. Sub-investment grade energy companies have been able to access the debt capital markets, but certainly at a premium as measured in higher yields. When credit tightens, sub-investment grade issuers may find they have limited access. Since the financial crisis of 2008 and 2009, credit availability has shrunk and has since improved. For some sub-investment grade issuers, the market substantially diminished as investors retrenched and funding tightened. Since 2008, most investment-grade issuers have not had difficulty accessing the debt markets.

In addition, the bond market has become a very important venue for certain national oil companies (NOCs). Some NOCs have tapped the bond market on an as-needed basis. Other NOCs have utilized the bond market on a regular basis and become serial issuers. These companies have ongoing financing needs that necessitate serial bond issuances. Unlike state-owned oil companies with hybrid capital structures (those that also have issued equity to outside investors), NOCs do not generally access the capital markets. There are exceptions. We will review instances of both situations.

Are the markets there for the smaller, more entrepreneurial alternative energy companies? Not always. For them, private placements may be a viable alternative. In this case, smaller, less-capitalized companies may choose to work with a smaller group of investors on a non-public basis. Public debt issuances are costly and require ratings by one of the rating agencies. A private placement may indeed also require a rating (or a rating letter) from one of the rating agencies for the investors. In either situation, the issuer pays for obtaining the rating.

PEMEX is a good example of an NOC that regularly frequents the global bond market. PEMEX is a financially savvy company that will wait for opportune moments to refinance higher interest rate bond issuances or come to the market with a new issuance. Investors know this company, and there is a substantial degree of transparency. PEMEX has an a very effective investor relations team and publishes a great deal of information to assist global investors.

Other large integrated majors can access the bond market. Their capital structures consist of senior debt issuances and, in some cases, commercial paper. Many large integrated majors have active commercial paper programs to augment shorter-term financing needs. These companies tend to have very high credit, typically A1/P1/F1 commercial paper ratings. While the commercial paper market is highly liquid, only the largest, most credit-worthy companies participate.

Equity Markets

Equity markets have proven to be friendly to both independent oil companies (IOCs) and alternative energy startups. The equity markets have also been accessible to smaller oil juniors in both the Canadian and UK stock exchanges. In addition, NOCs with hybrid structures have attracted equity investors looking for suitable opportunities.

Many oil juniors have completed initial public offerings on the Toronto Stock Exchange or London's AIM exchange. Both of these exchanges are small-company friendly, with teams of professionals to help smaller companies navigate the legal and regulatory hurdles.

Both the Toronto Stock Exchange (TSE) and London's AIM have proven to be successful launching grounds for several small- and micro-cap companies based in a variety of countries. The TSE has a distinct following of oil juniors doing business in Colombia and Peru. As such, there are numerous equity issuers doing business outside of Canada, but their stock trades on the TSE. Many of these smaller companies have opened offices in Canada to reach Canadian investors.

Brazil's Petrobras just raised approximately $70 billion in September of 2010 in a landmark equity offering. Petrobras came to the market amidst much media attention because of the dilutive effects the stock issuance would have on minority shareholders. While that may be the case, the fact remains that there isn't another single oil company with a plan to double production and grow the reserve base. Petrobras now sits on one of the largest crude oil discoveries just declared commercial in the newly named Lula field in the South Atlantic Ocean.

From an investment standpoint, the Petrobras story will take five to 10 years to play out. Its equity issuance played a big role in executing a complex transaction. The net effect was an increase in government ownership of its common shares. However, this company is now in an enviable situation among global oil majors. Few NOCs or IOCs have future access to eight or more billion barrels of oil equivalent.

The equity markets have and will continue to play an important role to both IOCs and hybrid capital-structure NOCs such as Petrobras or Norway's Statoil.

Investors

Who are today's investors in alternative energies, such as wind farms or hydroelectricity projects? Investors are varied and global. Today, everything from insurance companies, pension funds, and sovereign wealth funds will invest in energy projects. These investors will invest in infrastructure projects and alternative energy initiatives, as well as the more traditional form of bond or equity issuances.

In addition, hedge funds and private equity funds are actively investing in the energy sector. Hedge funds may take on somewhat passive investment roles, by purchasing the equities or bond issuances of both established and newer energy companies. New entrepreneurial companies may look to various private investors early in their life cycle. It is important for investors to bear in mind the duration of their investment. Public and private investments in the energy sector should be taken with a longer-term time horizon.

Venture Capital

Venture capital firms are a traditional form of financing for new, more entrepreneurial companies early in their life cycle. The roles of venture capital firms

FIGURE 4.1   Global Energy Sector M&A Activity relative to Deal Size (US$BN)

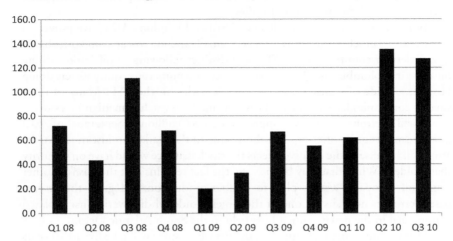

Source: Copyright © Capital IQ, Inc, a Standard & Poor's business. Standard & Poor's including its subsidiary corporations is a division of The McGraw Hill Companies, Inc. Reproduction of this Chart in any form is prohibited without Capital IQ, Inc.'s prior written permission.

vary widely. Some venture capital firms may insist on an active role in the company's management. Some firms may require that their representatives be placed on the board of directors. Others may participate in longer-range strategic planning and act more as a resource than as part of the management team. Figure 4.1 illustrates Global Energy sector mergers and acquisitions (M&A) activity by deal size through the third quarter 2010. The downturn in M&A activity was very apparent by the bottom of the commodity cycle in the first quarter of 2009. Energy sector M&A activity has since rebounded with the increase in crude oil prices.

Private Equity

While buying the stock or notes issuance may be of interest, an investor can indeed have a longer-term interest in the company. As such private equity investors take on a more active role by purchasing an interest in a myriad of energy companies. In return for their investment, many private equity firms will require either a key executive oversight role or a board-level position. This enables them to be closer to the decision making to protect their investment.

Private equity firms will typically have ownership stakes in a variety of companies. Some actively manage a broad portfolio of assets or some may have a sector focus. Private equity investors may play an important role for smaller, newer energy companies. Many funds have ongoing fundraising activities to facilitate intended acquisition stakes in target companies.

Sovereign Wealth Funds

Sovereign wealth funds have become a very significant part of the global institutional investor arena. Many countries have established sovereign wealth funds and invest in a variety of projects, stocks, bonds, and commodities. Sovereign wealth funds were established in Norway due to the long history of Norwegian oil production. Sovereign wealth funds have been established in Kuwait, Singapore, United Arab Emirates, and other countries.

Many sovereign wealth funds have a regional focus, seeking investment projects located in their backyards. There is a certain knowledge base and desire to support local projects. Other funds reach across the globe for infrastructure projects and other investment vehicles.

Figure 4.2 depicts the increase in M&A activity by number of transactions as crude oil and natural gas prices bottomed in first quarter 2009 and rebounded during 2010.

FIGURE 4.2   Global Energy Sector M&A Activity by Number of Transactions

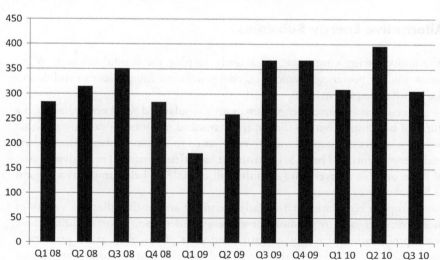

Large Institutional Investors

Pension funds and insurance companies are among the large institutional investors that may invest in energy projects or companies. These investors have money to put to work and often times seek worthy projects meeting their investment criteria.

Insurance companies may be limited to investments in certain jurisdictions as dictated by their credit committees and the National Association of Insurance Commissioners (NAIC). Insurance companies are highly regulated by the NAIC, which determines permissible investments. In other words, many projects or companies located in sub-investment grade countries will generally not meet a permissible investment profile.

Pension funds also have similar investment criteria. Pension fund managers have certain designated asset classes and percentage allocations where funds must be invested. Small- and mid-cap firms may fall within approved asset classes for some pension funds. Pension funds are less likely to invest in small- and micro-cap companies.

Hedge funds are active participants in the energy sector. Many will participate in smaller entrepreneurial energy firms or larger infrastructure projects. Hedge funds generally have specific investment criteria. Some hedge funds can invest significant amounts of capital in larger energy companies while others may be limited to considerably smaller investments.

Alternative Energy Subsidies

Alternative energy companies are actively tapping the capital markets. Wind farms, nuclear power companies, and coal generation companies can and do tap the bond and equity markets.

Recently, alternative energy sources such as solar and wind power have had a flurry of building activity as the United States and many European governments offered a variety of financial incentives designed to promote investment in alternative energy forms. The U.S. government has offered financial incentives as part of the economic recovery and stimulus bill of 2008 to help jumpstart a laggard U.S. economy.

European economies, particularly Germany and Spain, offered a variety of incentives designed to promote new energy generation. Prior to 2007, there was a proliferation of new wind farms and solar photovoltaic panel projects as governments offered lower tariffs, provided construction incentives, and issued building permits with relative ease.

As these economies embarked on muted economic recoveries, long-term subsidies began to dissipate. Power generators are left with cost structures that are quite different than originally planned. European subsidies disappeared as governments began to tighten the belt on spending. Many smaller wind farms and photovoltaic cell operators now find themselves in a situation with dwindling subsidies and cost structures that are under pressure.

Spain has become the poster child for governments that have retracted subsidies leaving power generators with unsustainable cost structures. The Spanish government is under intense pressure to reduce spending and rein in costs. Alternative energy subsidies have been cut back if not eliminated in many cases. Many alternative energy producers have closed their doors as costs are increasing with little to no government support.

The message is to be wary of the role subsidies play in alternative energy projects. If a project is built on subsidies, it is at risk. As soon as subsidies diminish (and eventually they all go away) a project can become vulnerable.

Concluding Thoughts

Energy projects have to be sustainable without government support. Energy projects and companies must be able to stand on the merits of the project and strong financial metrics. Investors have to be able to readily identify and manage the inherent business and financial risks associated with a project or a company.

Capital markets are vehicles for large, small, state-owned, and independent energy companies to access funds. Potential investors are encouraged to conduct due diligence, to investigate, and to amass broad knowledge of this very complex industry. In the end, we come back to strong balance sheets and sound financial metrics as these will always have investment appeal. In addition, a sound business model in a growth market makes for a solid, long-term investment strategy. Finally, be wary of the commodity cycle. By investing in companies or projects with strong balance sheets and cash flow stability, these institutions will be better able to withstand the downturns of the commodity cycle.

CHAPTER 5

The Quarterly Earnings Disconnect

Every quarter, we wait for the much-awaited earnings call, only to find several stock issues do not meet analyst's forecasts. Why do some energy stocks lag the rest of the market? While I appreciate the importance of quarterly earnings per share, I prefer to take the long-term view in the energy sector. This chapter reviews some of the more common issues associated with quarterly earnings, keeping in mind that nothing really transpires in a quarter in the energy sector. Therein lays the irony.

Short Term versus Long Term

Too often investors buy energy stocks with a short-term view. There isn't anything short term in nature about this industry. Whether it is drilling appraisal wells, building hydro projects, or establishing new solar photovoltaic power generation, these projects are by their very nature long term.

If investors are seeking near-term gratification, energy investments may disappoint the savviest investor. Short-term investors may be better served with retail, consumer products, or bank stocks, but not energy stocks. Securing financing for many alternative energy projects can take several quarters if not years. Power generation projects can similarly take years in the planning and financing phases, in addition to several years in the engineering and construction phases. Regulatory approvals and environmental permitting phases can also take years to obtain for power generation or oil and gas projects.

Therefore, I encourage patience and perspective in this sector. There is no such thing as immediate gratification, or immediate alpha, in energy. The complex and heavily regulated energy sector is not for those investors with a short-term time horizon. The investment time horizon must be longer term. If an investor is seeking gains and quick returns, within one to two quarters, the energy sector is sure to disappoint. Hence, understanding the nature of the beast helps us to identify those areas that best meet our investment objectives. Energy may well fit within the investment criteria of the fixed-income portfolio manager with a longer-term investment horizon.

Managing Expectations of the Street

To what extent does a given financial or operational metric meet or exceed the guidance established by management? Managing expectations is as much an art as a science. Because of the complexity of this industry, management has to carefully walk a fine line to not inadvertently misrepresent expectations or situations. Analysts must remember progress often moves at a crawl for any large infrastructure project. Certainly, it is essential to manage expectations, particularly in a quarter with disappointing earnings. Look for guidance on key operating and financial metrics knowing they have to be analyzed within the context of the commodity markets, competitors, and the broader industry.

Operational Metrics—Production Life Cycles

Crude oil and natural gas production life cycles take years to unfold. Early well testing and appraisal wells can take up to four years to assess investment and production potential. The process of developing first oil may take up to four years. While analysts look for continuous growth in crude or natural gas production, there are often minor production or supply disruptions. Theses disruptions are typically not of much concern. However, a production growth line may have some bumps associated with an upward trajectory.

The bid round process itself may take months, if not years, for some countries to realize. Hence, the industry often moves at a pace much slower than many investors' shorter time horizon. While the operational metrics of natural gas or crude oil production are important, one must view them within a wider context than quarter over quarter.

Similarly, natural gas and crude oil reserve growth takes years to unfold. While producers with securities are held to disclosure standards, posting significant gains in reserve growth is simply not realistic. The complexity surrounding reservoir modeling, geological testing, and assessing other technical data may take months or years to develop. We can look forward to new reserve certification disclosures on an annual basis. Producers will issue press releases on the commerciality of new fields when appropriate. The bottom line is that reserve growth will take years to materialize.

Restructuring Charges

During the downturns in the commodity cycle, many energy firms will begin to clean house, so to speak. A good example of this was the fourth quarter of 2008 and the first quarter of 2009 when both crude and natural gas prices plummeted and firms looked to shed unprofitable assets. In addition, write offs become more prevalent. Whether it is the decision to close a refinery, sell an interest in a block, or close a wind farm, the net effect is a restructuring charge. Economic downturns are often the precursor to financial restructuring charges.

Financial Considerations

There is no substitute for doing one's homework. And, as such, the energy sector is as complex as it gets. While no one can dispute the importance of quarterly earnings, the irony is that very little can actually get done within a single quarter of any given power, oil, gas, or alternative energy sector project. There is no doubt that investor's expectations are critical. Equally important is how the management of any of these energy companies guides investor expectations across a litany of projects that takes years to materialize.

Earnings and Margins

Every quarter we await earnings to analyze the changes, growth prospects, and risks that might have developed. Evidence of cost management and top-line revenue growth is the priority. Pressure on margins including gross margins, net margins, and earnings before interest, taxes, depreciation, and amortization (EBITDA) margins is readily apparent. Downturns in the commodity cycle will result in a decrease in all of the above-mentioned margins.

Table 5.1 illustrates the pressures on margins during an economic downturn across a sample set of 2,300 energy companies throughout the energy value chain. The data, courtesy of Capital IQ, aptly illustrates the effects in 2009 of a dramatic decrease in return on equity and return on capital. EBITDA and gross

TABLE 5.1 Profitability and Margin Analysis

Ratio	2006	2007	2008	2009	2010*
Return on Capital (%)	**13.9**	**11.8**	**11.9**	**6.5**	**11.7**
Return on Equity (%)	21.4	19.0	15.4	9.9	11.4
Gross Margin (%)	19.3	18.6	17.7	19.6	20.1
EBITDA Margin (%)	14.1	14.4	14.2	16.8	17.1
Net Income Margin (%)	6.9	6.7	7.7	6.9	6.7

Source: Copyright © Capital IQ, Inc, a Standard & Poor's business. Standard & Poor's including its subsidiary corporations is a division of The McGraw Hill Companies, Inc. Reproduction of this Chart in any form is prohibited without Capital IQ, Inc.'s prior written permission.
*Company Data as of LTM Sept. 30, 2010 on January 1, 2011

margins have already begun to improve with the economic recovery in 2010. Gross margins held steady throughout the downturn.

Liquidity—Cash Strategy

There is no substitute for a solid balance sheet. The mantra among many chief financial officers has been to maintain financial flexibility in these volatile times. As subsidies for alternative energy projects are diminishing in many countries, many alternative energy companies are finding themselves rebuilding and repairing balance sheets. Outside of North America and Europe, the appetite for wind and solar projects is steadily growing. However, many North American alternative energy CFOs are finding themselves preparing for the current softness in the market. The impact of weak natural gas prices and a soft global economy is being felt. As a result there are fewer wind and solar projects on the drawing board so long as there is a plethora of historically cheap natural gas.

Oil and gas producers are equally preserving their financial flexibility and building cash balances during the downturn in commodity prices. As crude oil prices have begun to climb, these companies with stronger balance sheets are now at a significant strategic advantage.

In addition, unused lines of credit and continuous access to the capital markets form the basis for financial flexibility. This is applicable to both small- and large-cap firms.

Dividends

Among large-cap energy companies, dividends have not been curtailed. Smaller-cap firms have had to make dividend adjustments as the economy dictated. As balance sheets are strengthening, dividends are being reinstated among small-cap firms. In many firms, a weaker-than-normal economy is an opportunity to revisit dividend policy. Decreasing a dividend is often the last resort. However, many mid-cap and smaller-cap firms are increasingly reviewing dividend policy. For larger power companies and integrated majors, dividends are considered on the generous side. Expect to continue to see the dividend status quo among the large-cap firms particularly in the current robust crude oil price environment.

Foreign Exchange—Currency Risk

Currencies continue to be a risk factor for many firms. Both large-cap and small-cap firms have exposure to a weaker dollar scenario. Firms are increasingly utilizing risk management strategies to mitigate such risk. As risk of U.S. inflation lingers, over the longer-term time horizon currency risk is going to increase. Over the next several quarters, the dollar will come under increasing pressure, resulting in upward momentum in commodity prices. Stronger emerging market currencies will result in continued growth abroad in the energy sector.

Share Buybacks

The strategy behind share buybacks generally is to increase the share price. Management may hold the belief that its shares are undervalued and begin a strategy to buy back shares. Energy companies that are flush with cash have begun buying back their own outstanding shares.

While share buybacks are fairly common, one might question whether there is a better strategy for excess cash. Large integrated majors are under increasing pressure to increase production and reserves. I am generally in favor of strategies that are targeted toward acquisitions, large or small, over share buybacks. Additionally, I favor initiatives aimed at increasing acreage, reserves, and production over share buybacks.

Cash Flow

The other key metric analysts assess is that of cash flow. In Chapter 3, we outlined some key metrics to help evaluate cash flows. On a quarterly basis, cash-flow fluctuations are readily apparent as commodity prices fluctuate. Operating cash-flow growth is paramount. Other cash-flow metrics include funds from operations or EBITDA. Always consider what is steady-state cash flow as opposed to cash flow boosted by temporary increases in commodity prices. Most companies will use a very conservative crude oil or natural gas price for their own internal planning and budgeting purposes.

Large- and small-cap firms will often participate in transactions that have off-balance-sheet accounting treatments. Again, the impact of acquisitions or divestitures will be readily apparent on a firm's cash flow.

Business Risks

Below are two business risks typically found within the energy sector. Certainly not all-inclusive, they illustrate two significant business hazards, that of regulatory risk and geopolitical risk. Legal risk has a very similar flavor to that of regulatory or geopolitical risk.

Regulatory Risk

Increasingly, regulatory risk is taking on a larger role in the energy industry. Whether a firm is an independent refiner or a power plant, regulation can and does have an impact on quarterly earnings. A recent example is that of the

Gulf of Mexico drilling moratorium on oilfield service sector firms. While the moratorium has been lifted, the effects are still being felt. Other countries, all over the globe, enact numerous policies that have earnings impact. Be wary of the bottom-line impact of increased regulation.

Geopolitical Risk

The energy industry is no stranger to geopolitics. Laws change all the time and some changes may be unfavorable to an energy company. Examples of this are the nationalizations of oilfield service sector assets in Venezuela. Geopolitics played a role in the nationalization of Venezuela's Orinoco Belt, resulting in the departure of two U.S. integrated majors. Given the dynamic of exploring and developing foreign oil and gas fields, geopolitical risk is present in many countries.

The most vivid example is the recent crude oil production shut down in Libya as a result of the internal unrest among various political factions. The biggest risk associated with Middle East turmoil is contagion. To date, protests in Bahrain, Yemen, Algeria, Oman, and Jordan have buoyed crude oil prices to levels not seen since the third quarter of 2008. A question here becomes one of exposure. Which companies have the most exposure and to what extent.

Pipeline and transport disruption are very real during political unrest. Some companies will be adversely impacted by pipeline disruptions and increased transport costs. Pipelines and tanker ships are frequently the targets of various troublemaking groups in certain countries amidst geopolitical unrest.

Concluding Thoughts

Quarterly earnings are but one piece of the total investment picture. The complexity of this industry warrants a much longer-term view than quarter-to-quarter earnings. While we all want quarterly earnings increases, perspective becomes very important. There isn't anything short term about the energy industry. There isn't any activity that will unfold during the course of a quarter.

We might be better served with a longer-term investment horizon. Energy infrastructure or alternative energy projects can take years to obtain environmental permits. Oil and gas companies can take up to four years before they produce first oil or gas in a newly discovered field. I believe there are worthwhile energy investments all over the globe. The message here is simply one of patience and perspective when investing in this complex sector.

PART II

Crude Oil and Natural Gas

51

CHAPTER 6

Analyzing Reserves

In the oil and gas industry, increasing reserves is one of the single biggest challenges among integrated majors. Increasing proven reserves is a key metric and one of the scorecards by which energy analysts measure exploration and development activity among oil and gas companies. Today, the challenge lies with the integrated majors and other independents to increase their reserve base when 79 percent (according to the Organization of Petroleum Exporting Countries [OPEC]) of the globe's reserves belong to national oil companies. Measuring reserves takes on critical importance as the valuation of these fundamental assets forms the basis of many financial decisions and investments.

Measuring reserves is highly technical and beyond the scope of this book. However, it is so important that we devote this chapter to a brief introduction with the hopes that interested investors, analysts, and others pursue additional learning in this fascinating area of the oil and gas industry.

The certification process fundamentally is the independent identification and measurement of the reserve base. This chapter addresses what is termed *proven reserves*, the bodies that develop the criteria, and an overview of the certification process.

Authorities on Reserves

Proven reserves criteria are developed by two authoritative bodies: the Society of Petroleum Engineers (SPE) and the U.S. Securities and Exchange Commission (SEC). The SPE is an industry professional organization that develops and advocates research and technology in the oil and gas industry. The SPE's involvement in quantifying reserves is logical, but one might wonder why the SEC has anything to do with oil and gas reserves. This simply is because any oil and gas company that issues securities in the U.S. markets must comply with SEC regulations aimed at protecting the investing public. The intent is to protect investors both large and small. Therefore, the SEC develops and sets reserve criterion that is very much aligned with that of the SPE.

Proven Reserves

The SEC has established definitions of what the industry refers to as proven reserves. Investors require comfort and assurance as to the quality and transparency of securities issued by oil and gas corporate issuers. Investors purchase corporate stocks and bonds of oil and gas companies (the issuers) who claim they have certain amounts of proven hydrocarbons as part of their asset base. Investors, bankers, and other constituents must have assurances as to the quality and quantity of the reserve base.

Reserves refer to the hydrocarbons still in the ground, including both oil and gas. Reserves are measured in terms of barrels of oil equivalent (BOE). Natural gas reserves must be converted to barrels and then added to the oil reserve base which is measured in terms of barrels. Natural gas reserves generally are measured in millions of cubic feet (mmcf). The industry convention is to multiply natural gas reserves by 6.0 to convert mmcf to barrels. The combination of natural gas and crude oil reserves is referred to as barrels of oil equivalent basis (BOE basis). This enables producers to compare all hydrocarbon deposits on an equivalent basis.

Industry Nomenclature

The oil and gas industry has established the convention of referring to the quality of reserves as 1P, 2P, and 3P. Proven reserves are known as 1P reserves. Those reserves categorized as proven and probable are 2P reserves. Those reserves which are deemed to be proven, probable, and possible are 3P reserves.

Table 6.1 refers to reserves which are deemed to be probable and possible, which are, by definition, considered unproven. As such, unproven reserves are categorized as 2P or 3P reserves. Every oil and gas producer will report its 1P,

TABLE 6.1   Reserves by Definition

Reserve Types	Definition
1P Reserves	Proven Reserves
2P Reserves	Proven and Probable Reserves
3P Reserves	Proven, Probable, and Possible Reserves

Source: U.S. Securities and Exchange Commission.

2P, and 3P reserves as part of its comprehensive annual financial disclosures with U.S. regulatory authorities. These disclosures will be in the annual report, 10K, 10-Q, and 20-F filings.

Why report 2P or 3P reserves if they are, by definition, unproven? Oil and gas producers report 2P and 3P reserves because they provide a picture as to future potential oil and gas reserve growth. In addition, 2P and 3P reserves provide a greater understanding and context of a given issuer's business. Over time, oil and gas producers will endeavor to convert 3P reserves into 2P reserves. Similarly, producers will try to convert their 2P reserves into 1P reserves by virtue of the certification process, which we will discuss later. Ultimately, the producer's goal is to convert unproven reserves into proven reserves.

Bankers, investors, and analysts view 1P reserves with much greater importance than 2P or 3P reserves. However, many oil and gas analysts will analyze and consider both 2P and 3P reserves to develop a complete picture of future growth and investment potential.

Proven Reserve Criterion

Proven, or 1P reserves, are those reserves which have a highly reasonable certainty or a 90 percent certainty of being recoverable under existing economic and political conditions, using existing technology. Under the category, proven reserves can be categorized as proven and developed reserves or proven and undeveloped reserves. Proven and developed reserves are those reserves which can be produced with existing wells or from additional reservoirs where minimal additional investment is required. Proven and undeveloped (PUD) reserves require additional capital investments such as drilling new wells to bring the oil to the surface.

The SEC acknowledges in Section 3. Definition of Proven Reserves: ". . . it is difficult, if not impossible to write reserve definitions that easily cover all possible situations. Each case to be studied as to its own unique issues." A summary of the SEC's criteria for proven reserves is found at: http://www.sec.gov/divisions/corpfin/guidance/cfactfaq.htm#P279_57537.

Reasonable Certainty

(a) Proved oil and gas reserves are the estimated quantities of crude oil, natural gas, and natural gas liquids which geological and engineering data demonstrate with reasonable certainty to be recoverable in future years from known reservoirs under existing economic and operating conditions, that is, prices and costs as of the date the estimate is made. Prices include consideration of changes in existing prices provided by contractual arrangements, but not on escalations based upon future conditions.

Existing economic and operating conditions is an important require-
ment. Producers must assess recovery techniques, operating costs, production methods, transport costs, marketing costs, ownership, and regulatory
requirements in effect on the date of the reserve estimate.

An oil and gas producer must be able to extract and develop hydrocarbons
within the existing economic environment. A producer cannot tell authorities
that hydrocarbons can be extracted and produced when crude oil prices reach
$90 per barrel. A producer has to be able to extract and produce the hydrocarbons
at the current oil prices.

An interesting example is that of Canadian oil sands. Not all Canadian
oil sands are economically viable at $30 per barrel. Some Canadian oil sands
become commercially viable at considerably higher crude oil prices. Therefore according to the SEC, "reserves attributed to the shut-in properties can
no longer be classified as proved and must be subtracted from the proved reserve data base as a negative revision. Those volumes may be included as a
positive revision to a subsequent year's proved reserves only upon their return to
economic status."

Hydrocarbons Still in the Ground

(b) Reservoirs are considered proved if economic producibility is supported
by either actual production or conclusive formation test. The area of a
reservoir considered proved includes that portion delineated by drilling
and defined by gas-oil or oil-water contacts, or both, if any, and the
immediately adjoining portions *not yet drilled*, but which can be reasonably
judged as economically productive on the basis of available geological and
engineering data.

In other words, proven reserves exist where hydrocarbons (oil or natural gas)
are currently in the ground. These reserves have not yet been extracted,
but there is sufficient technical and geological data to assess that they are economically viable.

Economical Viability and Existing Technology

(c) According to the SEC, reserves which can be produced *economically*
through applications of improved recovery techniques (such as fluid injection) are included in the "proved" classification when successful testing by a
pilot project, or the operation of an installed program in the reservoir, provides support for the engineering analysis on which the project or program
was based.

The SEC further states in Section 3 that, "if an improved recovery technique has not been verified by routine commercial use in the area is to be applied, the hydrocarbon volumes estimated to be recoverable cannot be classified as proved reserves unless the technique has been demonstrated to be technically and economically successful by a pilot project . . ."

For example, oil and gas producers cannot disclose that they will be able to extract hydrocarbons once the technology is developed in, for example, three years. The technology must be readily available today using their existing technology base.

Existing Wells

(d) Proved developed oil and gas reserves are reserves that can be expected to be recovered through existing wells with existing equipment and operating methods. The SEC goes on to include currently producing wells and wells awaiting minor sales connection expenditure, recompletion, additional perforation, or bore hole simulation treatment would be properties with proved developed reserves since the majority of the expenditures to develop the reserves has already been spent.

Unproven Reserves

Reserves may be estimated based on probabilistic methods and Table 6.2 is a high level guideline of such probabilities as they may be applied to reserves. Again, there is a significant amount of geological, legal, and technical testing to assess probabilities and official certification to reserves. Probabilistic methods include other guidance. Visit www.spe.org for technical definitions.

Unproven reserves are based upon geological and engineering data, similar to that used in estimates of proven reserves, but technical, contractual, or regulatory uncertainties preclude such reserves from being classified as proven. Issuers have the option of identifying their unproven reserves as either developed or undeveloped in their financial disclosures.

TABLE 6.2 Reserves by Recovery Probability

Reserves by Type	Recovery Probability
1P	90%
2P	50%
3P	10%

Source: U.S. Securities and Exchange Commission.

Old reserves that are shaped to known accumulations and claim a 50 percent confidence level of recovery are known as probable reserves and are included in 2P reserves, or proven and probable reserves.

Possible reserves are attributed to known accumulations which have a less likely chance of being recovered than probable reserves. As such, these reserves are deemed to have at least a 10 percent certainty of being produced. These reserves are known as possible reserves and are included in 3P reserves, or reserves which are proven, probable, and possible.

According to the SEC, Section 3, estimates of proved reserves do *not* include the following:

- Oil that may become available from known reservoirs but is classified separately as "indicated additional reserves"
- Crude oil, natural gas, and natural gas liquids, the recovery of which is subject to reasonable doubt because of uncertainty as to geology, reservoir characteristics, or economic factors
- Crude oil, natural gas, and natural gas liquids, that may occur in undrilled prospects
- Crude oil, natural gas, and natural gas liquids that may be recovered from oil shales, coal, Gilsonite, and other sources

There may be economic, geological, or reservoir characteristics that may preclude reserves from being designated as proven. This includes economic uncertainties such as a lack of a market or reserves that do not exhibit a positive cash flow.

Certification Process

The certification process becomes of strategic importance. Producers will work with a handful of highly specialized certification companies that analyze fields and reservoirs for commercial viability. The certification process is an independent audit process carried out by teams of geoscientists, petroleum engineers, and other experts aimed at assessing a given geologic structure for hydrocarbon potential.

The certification process utilizes technology that will measure fluid flow, pressure, and temperature under various conditions. The audit process will utilize three-dimensional (3-D) seismic and sophisticated reservoir simulation and computer modeling that will enable scientists to model a reservoir. The certification process is critical for oil and gas producers, or issuers, to obtain financing or access to the capital markets. Lenders and investors will require the independent audit of their reserve base in all key locations.

If an oil and gas producer issues securities in the United States, issuers must annually submit new reserves estimates to the SEC and publish this information in their publicly available financial disclosure documents. Every year producers begin with their year-end reserve base and add or subtract reserves depending on developments during the course of the year.

More on Reserve Authorities

There are two authoritative bodies in the industry that stipulate reserve criteria: The U.S. Securities and Exchange Commission and the Society of Petroleum Engineers. For U.S.-domiciled companies, they must follow the guidelines of the SEC. Corporations outside of the United States can follow the guidelines of the SPE. However, if any entity issues equities or fixed-income securities in the United States, it must also meet SEC guidelines. This applies to foreign corporations and the result is that most entities follow the criteria of both organizations.

Today, global markets necessitate that most corporations abide by both guidelines. Every oil and gas producer annually updates its proven reserves as well as its 2P and 3P reserves. This data is reported to industry authorities, such as the SPE and the SEC, and other financial reporting services for investors.

The U.S. Securities and Exchange Commission

The SEC permits oil and gas companies to now disclose both 2P and 3P reserves. The SEC liberalized the definition of proven reserves effective December 31, 2009, with the release of new reserve guidelines. The SEC record now recognizes that oil and gas companies have enhanced technical knowledge such as seismic mapping, enhanced recovery methods, and horizontal drilling to measure reserves of hydrocarbons. The SEC previously utilized an older definition of proven reserves that is more conservative in nature and did not recognize newer technologies that the industry has been utilizing for the last 20 to 30 years.

Analysts should always review all numbers that are reported by oil and gas companies under both the SPE and the SEC criteria. Today, proven reserves under both authoritative bodies should be very similar. Previously, there were minor discrepancies between the proven reserves of the SPE and the SEC. According to the SEC, the overview of the Oil and Gas Modernization can be summarized below.

Changes to Oil and Gas Definitions in Rule 4-10 of Regulation S-X

The new rules and amendments revise the current oil and gas definitions in Rule 4-10 of Regulation S-X as follows.

- **Average price:** The rules require the use of a 12-month average price—instead of a current single-day price (the current standard)—to calculate reserves to enhance comparability of reserves estimates among oil and gas companies, while reducing the effects of seasonality and short-term price volatility.

- **First-of-the month pricing:** The rules also direct companies to use first-of-the-month pricing to calculate the 12-month average to give companies more time to prepare estimates.
- **Reliable Technologies:** The rules permit the use of "reliable technologies" to establish reserve estimates instead of the current prescribed specific field tests. This extends the possible technologies permitted (previously specified) to establish reserves.
- **Nontraditional Resources:** The rules require that nontraditional resources (such as oil sands, bitumen, and shale) be included in oil and gas reserves instead of mining reserves because their products are essentially the same as those produced using traditional resources.
- **Eliminate "Certainty" Test:** The amendments change the definition of the term "proved undeveloped reserves" to use a "reasonable certainty" standard instead of a "certainty" standard, as required under the prior rules.
- **Supporting Definitions:** The rules also add and revise other definitions to the Commission's oil and gas reporting requirements for supporting terms used in the new definitions for proved, probable, and possible reserves—including a definition for the term "reserves."

In addition, other revisions to Subpart 229.1200, Item 1202 Disclosure of Reserves, includes disclosure on nontraditional resources such as bitumen, shale, and coalbed methane as oil and gas reserves. The regulation no longer specifies the technology used to establish reserves, requires disclosure of auditor qualifications, disclosure of third-party reports, and permits companies to disclose estimates of future prices. Item 1202 also permits, but does not require, disclosure of probable and possible reserves. Item 1203 (Proved Undeveloped Reserves) requires narrative disclosure of Proved Undeveloped Reserves (PUDs) to include the total quantity of PUDS, material changes, investments, progress, and explanations of PUDS that have remained undeveloped for five or more years.

This is not inclusive of every change to the regulation. As such, I encourage all investors and interested parties to read the new oil and gas reporting disclosures in its entirety at the SEC web site.

Society of Petroleum Engineers

The reserve numbers of oil and gas companies historically were typically very slightly higher under SPE criteria. The difference was often negligible. However, under the SEC's updated criteria, reserves numbers should be virtually identical. If an issuer discloses its reserve base under only one set of criteria, it has a tendency to raise questions. Most issuers will disclose reserve data under criteria from both the SEC and SPE.

Measuring Reserves

There are several methods of reviewing reserve data and drawing comparisons. Reserves can be measured in terms of years compared to production life. Reserves can also be measured in terms of the ratio of production to reserves. Finally, reserves can be measure in terms of a percentage.

Reserve to Production Ratio (Years)

A reserve-to-production-life ratio tells us how many years an entity can continue to produce oil or gas, at current production rates, before exhausting its existing reserve base. This ratio is measured in terms of years as illustrated in Table 6.3 crude oil reserves-to-production ratio. Iran has overtaken Saudi Arabia for the highest reserve-to-production ratio at 89.4 years .

Reserve Replacement

The idea behind reserve replacement ratios is that hydrocarbons that are extracted from the ground are replaced with new discoveries—with a given year. This is

TABLE 6.3 Crude Oil Reserves to Production Ratio

Country	2009 (years)
Iran	89.4
Saudi Arabia	74.6
Libya	73.4
Kazakhstan	64.9
Qatar	54.7
Nigeria	49.5
Gabon	44.1
Ecuador	36.1
Canada	28.3
United States	10.8
United Kingdom	5.8

Source: BP Statistical Review of World Energy June 2010.

easier said than done. Investors should look for institutions that have developed a track record in a 100 percent reserve replacement ratio, or a 1:1 ratio of barrels extracted to new barrels discovered. This is one of the single biggest challenges today in the oil and gas industry. Given that most of the globe's reserves are owned by state-owned oil companies, maintaining a 100 percent reserve replacement ratio is increasingly challenging for any independent oil and gas company. Table 6.4 illustrates crude oil reserves by number of barrels of oil.

Table 6.4 does not include the new unconventional natural gas shales found in both the United States and Canada. The chart does not reflect Canadian oil sands until they become proven reserves. It also does not include the newly declared fields of Lula in Brazilian waters. These are all newer developments and over the next several years we will see them added to their respective country's reserve base.

Reserves are one of the yardsticks by which the oil and gas industry measures itself. Table 6.4 displays which country is in a growth cycle and those that are stable to declining. Certainly, transparency becomes an issue with countries that are less open and I acknowledge that dilemma. In the industry, countries actively hire the certification and audit firms utilized by independent oil companies (IOCs). Venezuela is actively certifying its reserve base using reputable firms and by doing so its reserves are growing. Most countries are actively growing their reserve base with the hopes of less energy dependence on outside energy sources.

TABLE 6.4 Crude Oil Reserves (billions of barrels)

Country	1999	2009
Saudi Arabia	262.8	264.6
Venezuela	76.8	172.3
Iran	93.1	137.6
Iraq	112.5	115.0
Kuwait	96.5	101.5
United Arab Emirates	97.8	97.8
Russian Federation	59.2	74.2
Kazakhstan	25.0	39.8
Canada	18.3	33.2
United States	29.7	28.4
Brazil	8.2	12.9
Norway	10.9	7.1

Source: BP Statistical Review of World Energy June 2010.

Concluding Thoughts

Reserves are more than a scorecard in the oil and gas industry. Reserves are one of the end games. The goal is to continually increase reserves at or exceeding the pace of the current year of production. In other words, a company wants to replace a barrel of production with a new barrel that was discovered. This is one of the most significant challenges in the industry today. Given that the majority of the reserves are owned by national oil companies, the situation becomes increasingly more difficult for IOCs to keep building the reserve base. Finally, I would encourage interested readers to visit the SPE and SEC's websites for complete guidance and definitions. The complexity associated with defining reserves cannot be underestimated.

CHAPTER 7

Crude Oil Markets and Production

Over the past two decades, the crude markets have evolved significantly. No longer are the participants limited to the varied oil, gas, and other energy companies in the energy value chain. This chapter reviews some of the crude oil market participants that today include pension funds, hedge funds, global banks, and a myriad of other commodity trading organizations. The complexity has increased with financial institutions entering the arena that energy producers once dominated. This chapter also reviews the sometimes-volatile nature of the crude oil markets and the dynamics of its market pricing.

The Crude Oil Markets

Today, the regulatory environment has expanded both in terms of the crude markets with the Commodity Futures Trading Commission (CFTC) oversight as well as the plethora of environmental and governmental agencies' approval necessary to secure drilling permits. These agencies have proliferated and evolved amidst the need to ensure safety and protect the environment.

We begin analyzing key components of the crude markets and its relationship to crude oil production. The objective is to provide tools, terminology, and key operational metrics to help you perform your own analysis of the crude oil markets and conduct due diligence on crude oil producers.

Benchmark Crudes

What are benchmark crudes? Why is so much attention paid to crude oils such as the U.S. benchmark, West Texas Intermediate (WTI) or the North Sea crude oil

Brent Blend? These two crudes and other crude oils have a number of things in common critical to what is known as a benchmark crude oil. Benchmark crudes set the pricing standard by which other crudes can be measured or assessed. The benchmark crudes function as an index and provide a high level of transparency to investors and other market participants. The following are a few key criteria important to benchmark crudes.

Liquidity

Benchmark crudes have a significant amount of liquidity in the market. Prices can be obtained for both Brent and WTI virtually 24 hours per day, seven days per week. The breadth and depth of the market for these two crudes are substantial, with trading on international trading exchanges of the New York Mercantile Exchange (NYMEX) and the Intercontinental Exchange (ICE) in London.

Other crudes such as Dubai, Omani, Tapis, and Urals are also benchmarks for their given geographies. Buyers and sellers of physical crudes often price their cargos in terms of these other benchmark crudes. While Dubai crude is traded on the Dubai Mercantile Exchange, other benchmark crudes such as Dated Brent remain critical in pricing cargos in the physical market. The role of exchange-traded crude oil futures has expanded, enabling crudes such as WTI, Brent Blend, and Dubai to take on increased importance in their respective parts of the world.

Production

Benchmark crudes do not have production issues. These crude oils are not susceptible to production interruptions of any kind. Nevertheless, Brent crude is already in its natural decline. However, other neighboring fields such as Ekofisk, Forties, and several other crude oil fields exhibit the same crude characteristics. As a result, Brent Blend now includes a basket of other North Sea crudes, all with similar crude characteristics. There have never been any liquidity or production issues associated with Brent. Despite the fact that many of these North Sea fields are mature, North Sea crude producers are not sounding any alarms on production.

Geopolitics

Let it also be said that geopolitics cannot play a role in benchmark crudes. While geopolitics does play a significant role in the energy industry, among benchmark crudes there is no place for geopolitics. Whatever geopolitical event takes place, it can't impact benchmark crude production. For benchmark crudes, there must be ample crude supplies and a highly liquid market.

Inventory Levels

Crude oil prices are affected by many elements in the marketplace. Availability of crude oil supply is foremost among key drivers of price differences among different grades of crude oil. For example, Nigerian crude oil Bonny Light has a very desirable American Petroleum Institute (API) gravity of approximately 33.6 degrees. The benchmark crude oil—WTI—has an API gravity of approximately 38.7 degrees both API's are according to Energy Intelligence Group data. Which crude oil is priced higher? At first glance, one may be inclined to select a benchmark index crude such as WTI, but supply of Bonny Light is often challenged by disruptions in the transport process. As such, Bonny Light can occasionally command a higher price than WTI due to supply issues. Bonny Light is a relatively light sweet, low-sulfur crude with a high gasoline yield. As such, Bonny Light will occasionally trade at a premium to WTI or Brent crudes.

It is important to be aware of crude oil supplies in any market. This has considerable influence over crude oil futures markets. Twenty years ago, the relationship between crude oil inventories and crude prices was highly correlated. Today, it is less so. Why? Other factors are weighing heavily on crude prices such as global economic recovery, emerging market crude demand, and the effects of a weaker (or stronger as the case may be) U.S. dollar.

Among fundamental analysts, crude oil inventories are foremost. Currently, U.S. crude oil inventories are robust. After the financial crisis of 2008–2009, crude oil inventories have remained high, reflecting weaker-than-normal global crude demand. To date, WTI crude futures have traded beyond the $108-per-barrel mark, and Bonny Light broke through the $105-per-barrel barrier. Analyzing crude supply levels is critically important in assessing the demand picture. Globally, crude demand has been in the 88 to 89 mmbpd range. In recent years, the demand picture was on the weaker side. According to the Energy Information Administration (EIA), crude demand declined to approximately 83 to 86 mmbpd, reflecting sluggish Organization for Economic Cooperation and Development (OECD) economies in 2009. However, global economic recovery and Middle East turmoil has already buoyed crude prices to well over the $108 per barrel for WTI and $122 per barrel for Brent crude. New supplies of Canadian barrels entering the United States are keeping the supply of WTI crude at record-high levels, exacerbating the spread between WTI and Brent crudes, which has been in excess of $15 per barrel.

Crude Oil Quality

To the novice, crude oil differences may not appear to be wide and varied. However, crude oils are not created equal. While the chemical differences are complex, we will examine a few key differences among crude oils and their manifestation in pricing. Suffice it to say that a basic understanding of cost structures related to production is equally important in assessing investment opportunities.

Crude quality is driven by the location, depth, and many geological factors affecting a given crude oil. In other words, crude oils found in the North Sea are very different from crudes found in Venezuela's Orinoco Belt or Canada's oil sands. The chemistry and geology of crude oils are beyond the scope of this book, but suffice it to say that geology matters a great deal in the crude markets and production.

Crude oil can be identified and classified by the depth at which they are discovered. More specifically, crude oils are identified by the age of the source rock for a given reservoir. For example, crude found in the Paleozoic-era rock is approximately 250 to 570 million years old. Crude oils found in the Jurassic-age rock are approximately 145 million years old. The oldest crude oil can be found in source rock that dates from the Pre-Cambrian age and are generally older than 570 million years. In addition, crude oils vary by other chemical and geological factors such as viscosity, tan, gravity, pour point, and many other factors. The chemical analysis and behavior of every crude oil begins with the crude assay. Oil producers have teams of geologists, engineers, and other specialists that analyze crude oil under varying temperatures to determine the crude's yield. There will be more later on the concept of crude yield.

Crude Oil Markets

Twenty years ago, crude oil prices very diligently followed crude oil inventory levels. As inventories increased, crude oil prices dutifully decreased and vice versa. That simple relationship has been strained in recent years. Crude oil prices reflect many factors including inventory levels, economic growth, and other supply and demand factors. Increasingly, crude oil prices today are following the performance of the equity markets. In addition, crude oil prices are impacted by currencies. We'll have a look at each of these market dynamics and try to put it in a rational framework.

Market Participants

Over the past two decades, crude oil markets have evolved considerably. No longer are producers in the energy value chain the primary buyers and sellers of crude and refined products. Today, the institutional investor market consists of participants not only in the crude and natural gas futures market, but in the physical side of the industry.

Large global banks in particular have filled a need or a void in the industry for commercial users of fuels. Where traditional oil and gas companies have chosen not to participate in the commercial side of the business, banks have entered with gusto. The banks are helping large commercial users of fuels hedge and implement risk-management strategies. The commercial side reflects the needs of large users of fuels such as transport companies, airlines, and others who need to actively hedge their exposure to crude or natural gas price fluctuations, and the large global banks have aggressively filled that need.

The Equity Markets

In recent years, crude oil prices have exhibited what appears to be a stronger correlation to stock market movement than fundamentals such as supply, demand, and inventory levels. The Standard and Poor's (S&P) 500 and broader market indices have become proxies for broader energy market demand. Since the stock price of corporations that comprise the stock market indices move up and down in anticipation of increased or decreased future market demand for their goods and services, energy prices will follow suit driven by the expected increased or decreased demand for energy needed to produce and consume those goods and services. As the global economy improves or contracts, the effects play out in equity and commodity indices.

Commodity markets will react to the movement of the equity markets reflecting expected demand or lack thereof for commodity products. This phenomenon will play out in other commodities such as natural gas, metals, or other commodities impacted by broader manufacturing and industrial performance. An excellent current example is relatively weak North American energy demand and the prospects of increased supply that has resulted in weakening of natural gas prices.

Market Fundamentals

Crude oil prices are also impacted by fundamental supply, demand, and energy market production disruptions. Global supply and demand are essential to crude oil price movement and understanding market behavior. Even though global economies are improving and demand is recovering, inventory levels are still considered fairly robust, particularly in the U.S. market. Figure 7.1 depicts U.S. crude oil inventories, still above the five-year average. As such, WTI pricing has reacted to this inventory build-up and has not kept pace with Brent crude pricing which has pierced the $122 per barrel mark.

Supply Disruptions

Crude oil prices are very much impacted by pipeline or refinery production disruptions. A major refinery outage can result in spot market price increases of

FIGURE 7.1   EIA Crude oil Inventories (mm barrels)

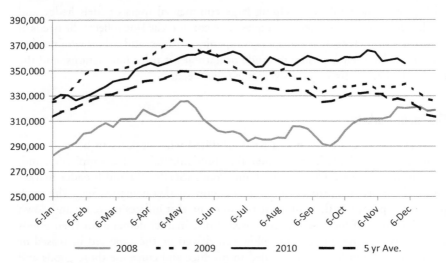

Source: U.S. Energy Information Administration (EIA).

$1 to $2 per barrel. Similarly, a major pipeline disruption can also result in a similar increase in the spot market for crude prices. During 2010, France was adversely impacted by numerous strikes resulting in supply disruptions to major refineries, including the Dunkirk refinery and others. Spot market prices for refined products increased in many European markets. Middle East turmoil and Libyan production disruptions are other examples that have placed pressure on near-term pricing particularly Brent crude prices.

Crude Yield

Every barrel of crude oil has what is referred to as its yield. The yield is, on a percentage basis, the portion of the crude that can be produced into all of its various refined products under specific conditions. These refined products include gasoline, diesel fuels, naphtha, residuals, jet fuels, and asphalt. The crude yield has a lot to do with differences in crude prices.

For example, heavier crudes such as Mexican Maya have a very different yield than that of a North Sea Brent Blend. As such, these two crudes command different prices. For example, Brent crude produces a higher yield of diesel and gasoline. Mexican Maya produces a higher yield of heavier diesels and other heavier refined products. Gasoline and the middle distillate cut (various grades of diesel fuels and gasoils) are the most valuable refined products. Therefore, Brent blend and Maya have very different prices in the market on any given day. As such, Maya may have an $8 to $10 per barrel discount to Brent blend.

Transport costs are the other variable that impact market pricing of crudes. Crudes are transported via pipeline, tanker, rail, and tanker truck. Globally, crude will be transported via large tanker ships. Pipeline is still the most economical method for transporting crudes and refined products. Crude transport costs play a role in the daily decisions of investors, commercial users, and producers as to whether to purchase light, sweet crudes that are moved via pipeline versus heavier, sour crudes transported by tanker ship.

Refining Considerations

The refining process is an important consideration in any study of crude oil production and markets. In Chapter 9, we'll more closely review the importance of refining. For the moment, let us accept that not all refineries are created equal. This is an important consideration in assessing pricing, investment decisions, and demand profiles for various crudes.

Of strategic importance is the quality of refining assets. The integrated majors generally have world-class refining assets. This means they are able to refine heavier crude oils into the more valuable products such as diesels and gasoline. Many of the majors have key refining production units such as hydrocrackers, catalytic crackers, and cokers that are necessary to refine heavier crudes such as Cold Lake Blend to produce gasoline and diesel. Therefore, a careful assessment of the downstream asset infrastructure is essential to good due diligence.

Gasoline

Gasoline demand reflects a certain amount of seasonality in its pricing structure. The northern hemisphere's summer driving season in Europe and North America is the primary seasonal factor generating increased demand for gasoline. Figure 7.2 illustrates U.S. gasoline inventory levels that have been high relative to the five-year average. As China's demand for refined products grows, refined fuels imports into China will have a considerable bearing on crude oil prices. Analysts should track global gasoline demand, import, and export levels to ascertain direction of the market. This is only one component of many variables.

Distillates

Distillate demand largely reflects seasonality in winter months in portions of the northern hemisphere where home heating oil is still in use. However, there is considerable seasonal demand from agribusiness, where diesel fuels power tractors, combines, and other heavy machinery. Users of the middle distillate fuels

FIGURE 7.2   EIA Gasoline Inventories (mm barrels)

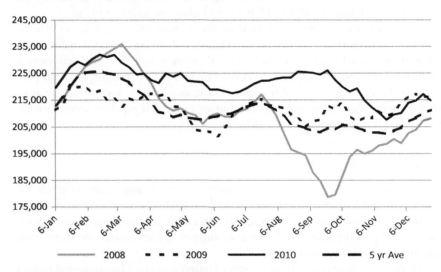

Source: U.S. Energy Information Administration (EIA).

include railroads, marine transport, truck transporters, and, of course, suppliers of home heating oil. Since 2008, U.S. distillate inventory levels reflect very sluggish demand and, as of 2011, are still very much above their five-year average.

Quality Differential

There is what is called a heavy/light differential or a sweet/sour differential. This spread captures the economic reality that crude oil prices vary by quality and traders often used this information to buy or sell from a higher priced location to a more inexpensive one. Quality makes a considerable difference for producers that tend to refine more of the heavier sour crudes. As the spread between the heavy and light crude oil narrows, profitability for the heavy producers improves. The spread between crude qualities is an important distinction for investors to monitor.

Location Differential

The costs of moving and transporting crude oils vary across the globe. The prices associated with moving crudes will, to some extent, drive prices for a given crude oil. There are days when Bonny Light is actually trading and pricing higher than Brent and WTI. What we need to consider is that Bonny Light, a Nigerian low sulfur, light sweet crude oil is often times the subject of pipeline disruptions and supply issues. As such, Bonny Light can actually trade higher than Brent or WTI. Location and transport costs matter a great deal in the crude markets.

Transport costs will often influence pricing of a crude oil. The most economical means for moving a crude oil is by pipeline. However, if a crude oil is being transported by a VLCC (very large crude carrier) tanker on a specific route, this crude may price higher, on a per barrel basis, simply because of transport costs.

Spot Market versus Futures Market

Refined products can be physically obtained in the spot market or as they say in the industry "the rack." The spot market refers to the terminals where product is priced and delivered, typically within a 30-day time frame. Purchasers of products can price and pick up refined products at a local terminal. This is the case for jet fuel, diesel fuel, and gasoline commercial users.

The rule here is that activity in the spot market will influence the futures market. Because this premise generally holds true, large commercial users of fuels are able to hedge their purchases of fuels. For example, a disruption in a pipeline or long-term refinery outage can affect the futures markets for gasoline or distillates in at least the front month.

Futures market pricing generally impacts product priced beyond the 30-day time horizon. Buyers and sellers of crude and refined products can look to the futures market for guidance in the direction of the forward curve. A forward curve where the near-term months are priced lower than outer months is referred to as a contango market. A forward curve with higher near-term prices than outer months is referred to as a backwardated market.

Effects of Government Policy on Crude Markets

We conclude this chapter by acknowledging the considerable effects that government policy and the currency markets have on crude markets. As governments continue to adopt policies of increasing stimulus, implement what is termed *quantitative easing*, and weaken reserve currencies, price inflation can and will ensue. Consequently, commodity prices will immediately react and begin to move northward. This is very apparent in gold, silver, metals, and energy markets. As the U.S. dollar decreases relative to the Euro, crude oil prices creep up.

There is a very definitive cause-and-effect relationship with regard to the strength of the dollar and future inflation expectations. The groundwork is already being laid for near-term increases in commodity prices including the energy complex. In addition, crude oil prices have already reached triple digits due to Middle East geopolitics, increases in demand, production uncertainty, and yes, the fear premium. Perhaps crude prices will not stay in the triple digit range on a sustained basis. We must remember that commercial and industrial crude demand can and will retrench when crude prices begin to flirt with $120 per barrel.

Concluding Thoughts

Today, crude oil markets have rebounded with a vengeance. Brent crude has already surpassed $122 per barrel and WTI is holding firm in the lower $108 range. Emerging market economic growth is behind much of the increase in price as Chinese demand for commodities such as gasoline and crude continue to climb.

At this juncture, it doesn't appear that Organization of Petroleum Exporting Countries (OPEC) countries will increase production, given that crude oil inventories are still relatively high and above the five-year average levels. Certainly, $110 per barrel crude has already been breached by many Asian crudes. Brent crude is near $122 per barrel and WTI is already having its day in the spotlight. Given the wide disparity between WTI and Brent, WTI is losing is lustre as a benchmark crude. Over time, WTI may evolve into only a key regional North American benchmark crude.

Are we in a bubble market? Only time will tell. What is certain is the adverse affect that extreme energy prices have on commercial users of fuels. History could repeat itself. In the third quarter of 2008, commercial users of fuels retrenched after crude prices reached $130 to $147 per barrel as cost structures were adversely affected. By the fourth quarter of 2008, crude oil demand collapsed resulting in a dramatic decrease in crude oil prices to $35 per barrel heralding in the so-called Great Recession. This is a situation where the current crude oil markets are treading in precarious waters.

CHAPTER 8

Natural Gas Markets and Production

The most significant development in the natural market is the expectation of what is about to take place over the next five to ten years. The U.S. market is undergoing nothing short of a natural gas boom with the potential development of unconventional natural gas shales.

In this chapter, we will explore both the conventional and unconventional natural gas production. This is not a chapter on drilling or hydraulic fracturing, but an overview of natural gas pricing economics. In addition, we will review the important market dynamics associated with the natural gas markets.

We dedicate a portion of this chapter to the unique structural requirements and behaviors of the U.S. natural gas market. The U.S. gas market behaves unlike other geographies where natural gas prices are regulated by local governments. Elsewhere, natural gas is a utility and, as such, prices to the public are regulated, capped, and kept from skyrocketing the way they can in the United States.

De-Coupling of Natural Gas from Crude Oil

Let's begin by examining natural gas price behavior relative to that of crude oil prices. Once upon a time, crude oil prices were highly correlated to natural gas prices. If crude oil prices increased or decreased, so did natural gas prices. After all, both natural gas and crude oil are hydrocarbons found in similar reservoirs and surfaced using similar drilling techniques. They are often extracted together, incurring similar pricing and cost structures. Not so fast. Today, that's where they begin to diverge.

In terms of market pricing, the most significant decoupling of natural gas pricing began in 2008 after the financial crisis. During the bull run of the crude oil markets in 2006 to 2008, U.S. natural gas prices increased in lock step with crude oil prices. When crude oil prices plummeted in the third quarter of 2008, U.S. natural gas prices fell as well. However, while crude oil prices began to rebound in 2009, U.S. natural gas prices remained very lackluster. The market did not see a rebound in natural gas prices.

Not only have supplies of natural gas been more than healthy, but demand for U.S. natural gas has not by any means been stellar. Among the commercial, industrial, and residential sectors, demand for natural gas has been weak, reflecting the muted recovery taking place in the United States and Europe. In addition, as previously mentioned in this chapter, the U.S. market is undergoing nothing short of a natural gas boom. The potential reserves associated with unconventional natural gas plays are staggering. The U.S. market could be up for natural gas self-sufficiency easily for the next decade, with reserve potential that could double or triple current reserve levels.

In addition, the increase of natural gas reservoirs or these unconventional shale plays add to the potential future increased production and reserves. Production is expected to increase over the mid-term, adding to already increased inventories. Reserves will likely grow over the next decade as well, as these basins are certified as proven reserves. Hence, the race is on by natural gas producers to add to their acreage.

Recently, we have witnessed a weakening in U.S. natural gas prices as all of these unconventional shale plays come to light. While crude oil prices have bounced back, natural gas prices are still trailing behind in the $4.50 per million British Thermal Units (mmBtu). The price divergence is likely to remain.

It is important to note that natural gas pricing tends to be very unique to its market. In Europe, natural gas prices are more robust in the $7 per mmBtu range. In other markets, natural gas prices are regulated and capped, protecting the public from market swings in pricing.

Conventional Natural Gas Production

Conventional natural gas production largely mirrors traditional crude production using conventional drilling methods into reservoirs typically having large pockets of natural gas in geologic structures known as traps. These traps vary by geology, but are characterized by pockets of natural gas that may or may not be above a layer of crude oil.

It is important to note differences in natural gas; hydrocarbons found with crude oil are "associated natural gas" and those found without crude oil are "non-associated natural gas." A given reservoir may contain strictly natural gas such as those referred to later in the chapter.

Unconventional natural gas shale plays utilize a hydraulic fracturing method that has been in use for many years, which we'll discuss later. According to Hydraulic Fracturing (www.hydraulicfracturing.com), this production method utilizes various drilling fluids including water, sand, and other additives that are pumped at extremely high pressures down a wellbore. The liquid fractures the sedimentary rock where natural gas exists in small pockets deep into these rock layers. While the geology is beyond the scope of this book, it is important to note the differences in production and costs associated with each type of drilling.

North American Unconventional Natural Gas Shale Plays

The potential growth in the unconventional natural gas shale plays in the U.S. and Canadian markets have the ability to secure energy sources for a decade in North America. Over the next decade, the potential reserves associated with these shale plays could triple the existing U.S. reserve base.

Essentially, current reserves of nearly 200 tcf (according to the Energy Information Administration [EIA]) could top 600 tcf over the next decade. This situation has resulted in a race to acquire acreage in the U.S. market. Every integrated major along with many smaller independents are quickly forming partnerships to acquire acreage. In addition, several global majors are vying for positions as well. From India's Reliance to France's Total, and everyone in between, energy companies are acquiring basins and acreage as well as making corporate acquisitions to tap into this market.

One of the most significant concerns that will be resolved prior to commercial development is the safety of the hydraulic fracturing method of extracting these hydrocarbons. At issue is whether the drilling process has the potential to contaminate underground water tables. New York has already banned all hydraulic fracturing in the state. Other states are reviewing the technology's safety record.

The hydraulic fracturing process uses water, other drilling fluids, and sand at very high pressures to break thousands of feet of sedimentary rock. The oil and gas industry is conducting studies and research to determine potential hazards and the U.S. Environmental Protection Agency (EPA) is also reviewing the technology to determine whether water tables would be adversely impacted. The jury is still out.

Even though the enabling technology of hydraulic fracturing has not yet been sanctioned, many companies have begun the process of acquiring other companies with technological know-how or acquiring companies with significant acreage or a presence in this market. Figure 8.1 depicts the majority of proven shale reserves in the lower 48 states in the United States. Acquiring technology has quickly become of strategic importance to many producers.

What is the net result? Today, there is minimal impact. The question is how does this potential reserve shift impact future pricing? While none of us has a crystal ball, it is a safe assumption that future natural gas pricing could be soft. Notwithstanding the fact that natural gas is a cleaner fuel, demand is lackluster; we need to look to overall economic growth to boost fuel demand.

FIGURE 8.1   U.S. Natural Gas Shale Reserves 2009

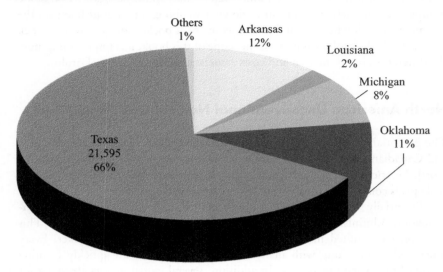

Source: U.S. Energy Information Administration (EIA).

Therefore, I anticipate softness in the near- to mid-term natural gas market. Longer term, I see more robust natural gas pricing as more power producers begin the shift to natural gas. This will unfold over the next decade as power generation producers, particularly in Asian countries, begin to build natural gas infrastructure. For example, China is still a huge user of coal due in part to the lack of pipeline infrastructure to transport natural gas. I anticipate this market dynamic will change, but it will take the better part of a decade to materialize.

Canadian Natural Gas Markets

Like the United States, Canada holds significant reserves in the unconventional shale plays throughout the country. These reserves are part of the North Dakota play known as the Bakken. The Canadian side of the Bakken is as prolific as the United States as these shale gases extend northward into Canada. The provinces of Alberta and British Columbia have several shale plays including the Horn River and others.

In the current environment, Canadian natural gas producers face the same challenges as U.S. producers do. Historically depressed natural gas prices are preventing producers from developing unconventional shales. In other cases, current weak natural gas prices are also beginning to impact the conventional side of the market. Producers are slowly beginning to curtail production as natural gas inventory levels are robust. As production begins to slow, prices may slowly begin to increase. The weak natural gas market is being felt in other energy streams such as the alternative energy market.

Natural Gas Markets

Natural gas pricing is impacted by weather, transport costs, supply, and demand. There is a very clear and definite seasonality to the natural gas markets in the Unites States and Europe. If we know the geography, we can construct the supply and demand picture. As such, one of the most telling pieces of data that followers of the market should seek is the Weekly Underground Storage Report distributed by the U.S. Department of Energy on the EIA's web site.

This report depicts, by U.S. region, the status of natural gas weekly storage. As you might expect, this data reflects the inherent seasonality associated with North American natural gas markets.

European natural gas markets tend to behave similarly to U.S. markets with the UK natural gas market at the forefront. Storage levels, seasonality, and weather are primary drivers of the U.S. and European natural gas markets. Currently, UK natural gas prices reflect a far more robust market with prices in the $7 per mmBtu range. Unlike UK markets, U.S. natural gas prices have not broken through the $4.50 per mmBtu mark for most of 2010. Figure 8.2 illustrates the weakening of natural gas prices since the market high of 2008.

FIGURE 8.2 U.S. Natural Gas Futures Prices

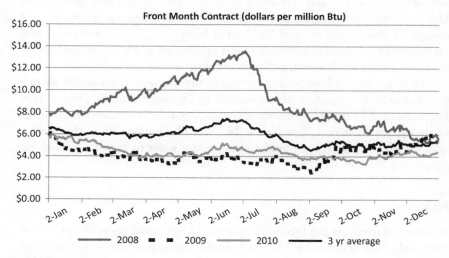

Source: Bloomberg.

Pricing Hubs

Because of the unique nature of the U.S. natural gas market, we devote some space to an overview of this complex market. The U.S. market is structured using the concept of pricing hubs, whereby major cities are designated as pricing hubs. The concept here is that natural gas prices in the spot or physical market differ by city or pricing hub. For example, natural gas prices in New York City are not the same as Florida, or Houston, or anywhere on the west coast. The primary differences are in transport costs, seasonality, underground storage levels, and weather.

For example, if natural gas prices at the New York City gate are $4.87 per mmBtu, natural gas prices in Houston may be $4.50 per mmBtu. Every pricing hub will be slightly different and reflect the economics specific to that pricing hub. Each pricing hub primarily reflects the transport costs it takes to move natural gas from point A to point B and weather-related demand in different locations.

The term that is used in the industry is "basis." The basis is simply the pricing differential from one location to another measured relative to the NYMEX for U.S. markets. For example, the basis for the New York City hub might be $0.50 per mmBtu. This means it is priced $0.50 per mmBtu higher than the benchmark Henry Hub pricing. If the New York City gate basis was ($0.50) per mmBtu, this would signify that the New York City gate's basis was less than Henry Hub pricing. Henry Hub in Erath, Louisiana, is the delivery point for the NYMEX natural gas futures contract—a benchmark for the fuel.

Weekly Underground Storage

Currently, U.S. natural gas inventories are near historic highs partially due to lackluster commercial and residential demand. Over the last two years, as the U.S. economy slowed, so did demand for natural gas. Consequently, natural gas storage (or inventories) reached 3.837 tcf in November 2009 as demand waned for natural gas. Typically, hurricane season in the Gulf of Mexico whittles down natural gas stock levels and that did not occur in 2010.

Northern hemisphere autumn ushers in the withdrawal season for natural gas. Typically, the injection period is April to October. According to the U.S. Department of Energy, U.S. inventories typically peak in November when storage reaches approximately 3.50 trillion cubic feet. The implication is that weekly underground storage reports need to stay on our radar to monitor natural gas supply and demand.

Production

At current natural gas production rates in the U.S., natural gas prices will, more than likely, have to dip below $3.25 per mmBtu before producers begin to curtail production levels. The current glut of natural gas is keeping a ceiling on U.S. natural gas prices while natural gas prices on the other side of the Atlantic are much more robust. Within the current environment, unconventional natural gas shale producers are waiting for more favorable economics before developing and producing these shale plays. While the cost structures vary from producer to producer, generally most natural gas producers are waiting for natural gas prices to return to $6 to $7 per mmBtu to develop unconventional shale plays.

International locations

Natural gas pricing takes on different forms in other geographies. Many countries, including some Asian and Latin American countries, have price caps on natural gas pricing at the commercial and industrial, as well as at the consumer levels. In general, the motive behind these pricing philosophies tends to be political in nature. This prohibits producers from increasing prices on the electorate. The result is that producers increasingly curtail investments in these countries because they cannot earn an adequate rate of return. No one benefits from this cycle of under-investment, but it is a stark reality of operations in countries with regulated prices.

LNG—Fuel for the Future

In this chapter, we dedicate attention to a very important area of natural gas development: liquefied natural gas (LNG). Over the last several years, LNG's promise has significantly risen as countries that had natural gas shortages seek LNG as an energy alternative. While the transport and storage infrastructure becomes a critical part of tapping into this energy source, access to water is essential. For countries that are not landlocked, LNG has become a viable alternative energy source.

For those new to LNG, the idea is to transport liquefied natural gas from offshore installations and transport it to shore via pipeline. According to Chevron (www.chevron.com), the LNG is then stored in a facility where it is chilled and the natural gas transforms to a liquid hundreds of times smaller than its original size. According to Chevron, LNG is chilled to temperatures of $-162°C$ ($-260°F$). The LNG is then stored and transported via specially insulated LNG ships to various locations around the globe. LNG ships are double-hulled and heavily insulated to ensure temperature control. When the LNG arrives at its destination, the LNG is warmed at import or re-gasification terminals back to its original gaseous state. The natural gas is then sent via pipeline for commercial, industrial, and residential use.

Natural Gas Storage

Natural gas is often stored in underground salt domes and aquifers. These salt domes are depleted reservoirs that previously held natural gas, or in some cases crude deposits, and today hold natural gas. These underground storage caverns are scattered throughout the United States primarily in the Midwest and the Texas-Oklahoma-Arkansas corridor.

The important thing regarding storage is twofold: During the summer months, producers are inputting natural gas reserves into storage and ramping up for the upcoming winter months. This process of inputting reserves is what is known in the industry as "injections" into the system. Conversely, when local distribution companies begin to extract natural gas out of storage, this process is known as "withdrawals" from storage.

As previously mentioned, natural gas usage is very much driven by weather and seasonality. Investors and energy analysts track weekly storage levels throughout North America and Europe to ascertain demand levels. In addition, storage levels will greatly impact market pricing. U.S. and Canadian natural gas storage levels are fairly robust while European storage less so. UK natural gas prices are much more in balance for producers, while North American natural gas producers are at the low point of the commodity cycle.

Natural Gas as a Utility

In the United States, natural gas is governed by the Federal Energy Regulatory Commission (FERC). FERC is the governing body in the natural gas, natural gas storage, and pipeline sectors of the energy industry. It is important to note what FERC does and does not do. FERC sets tariffs and pricing throughout the industry. Local distribution companies simply cannot charge the public without having made their case before FERC. In other words, profitability is very much regulated in the natural gas utility world.

As a result of various FERC orders, pipeline companies became strictly transport companies. In other words, the pipeline companies do not own the hydrocarbons. They simply transport the molecules. Pipeline transport is a process that is extremely complex and takes place like clockwork through the nominations process. Essentially, producers of natural gas make arrangements with pipeline companies to transport their gas through the pipeline structure at certain times and dates. The window for initiating the nominations process typically takes place at the end of the month. Transporters will charge fees based on volume and distance. In most countries, the transport network is governed by local natural gas regulators. Profitability to local distribution companies and pipeline companies is heavily regulated.

Natural Gas—The Cleaner Fuel

Natural gas is considered the cleanest of the fossil fuels. Natural gas has 45 percent fewer carbon dioxide (CO_2) emissions that any of the other fossil fuels. In addition, natural gas has 90 percent fewer emissions of oxides of nitrogen and sulfur than the current state of today's coal technologies.

As such, I believe the natural gas market is going to improve in the coming years. Today, the natural gas market in North America is very weak. The impact is being felt in numerous ways. Longer term, natural gas is going to be a very good investment story. As the power sector begins to move away from coal, natural gas becomes an excellent alternative. Infrastructure becomes the key to expansion of natural gas usage in countries like China and Russia which are currently not significant natural gas users. Building infrastructure will take the better part of a decade in China and Russia.

Nowhere else is the impact of a weak natural gas market being felt than in the alternative energy sector of wind and solar energies. The weak natural gas market has meant the cost of utilizing natural gas has certainly decreased. Meanwhile, prices for alternative energy sources such as solar and wind have remained high relative to natural gas. This has had a dampening effect on current wind and solar investment projects. This will only change as wind and solar energy technologies become more economically competitive with natural gas.

Concluding Thoughts

Energy companies all over the globe are watching this industry game changer unfold and are eager to participate in North American unconventional natural gas shales. Despite the current weak environment in natural gas pricing, I am bullish on natural gas as a fuel source. The cleaner burning aspects make this fuel choice very attractive. The unconventional shale formations in North America present a significant opportunity to secure the energy supply for the next decade.

Also, developments in LNG make natural gas available in markets that experienced shortages of natural gas. LNG is a viable alternative that is expected to grow. The 2011 Japan nuclear crisis will also result in renewed interest in LNG for countries that are not landlocked. LNG is going to have its day in the spotlight over the near and midterm.

CHAPTER 9

Understanding Refining Economics

The U.S. refining landscape has changed dramatically. In this chapter, we explore the specifics of how and why refiners continually face a challenging environment. We begin with a review of industry structure and the business model. We also review some key economic metrics important to refiners and critical to understanding the economics of the refining process. Finally, we review the challenges and state of the refining industry and assess its outlook.

The Business Model

As previously discussed, the integrated oil business model consists of exploration and production (E&P), midstream segment, and downstream operations. Downstream business operations generally consist of retail gasoline operations. Most integrated majors will include refining operations in what is broadly referred to as the downstream segment. Within the midstream segment there may be terminal operations, pipelines, and other product-finishing and transportation operations.

In the oil industry, there are companies that focus exclusively on midstream or downstream operations and don't have E&P operations. A few of these companies are what one might refer to as independent refiners, focusing only on refining operations and perhaps some retail operations. These refiners don't have the diversification of E&P operations to expand their earnings. As a result, their earnings are completely dependent on refining economics which are often times mediocre at best.

In an integrated oil business model, business losses incurred in the downstream segment are frequently offset by profitable E&P business segments. Most integrated majors expect that downstream operations will often times have poor or negative refining margins. Within the integrated model, the downstream business segment often posts poor earnings quarter after quarter. The independent refining company does not have the benefit or cushion of a diversified earnings stream.

Challenge for Independent Refiners

Independent refiners are subject to the vagaries of crude oil prices and are experiencing, to put it mildly, challenging times. Independent refiners are particularly vulnerable to crude prices simply because they purchase crude oil at market prices to refine. Unlike integrated majors, independent refiners are not refining their own equity crude oil. Independent refiners are purchasing crude oil, often times 30 days or more in advance of when the crude oil will be delivered, refined, and later sold. Therein lays the challenge for many independent refiners.

If a barrel of crude is bought at $80 per barrel and 20 to 30 days later it is refined and ready to be sold, crude oil prices have now moved. The challenge becomes have prices moved in the right direction, benefitting refiners, or an adverse direction, further eroding margins. Refiners have to layer in transportation costs, taxes, quality differentials, and so on, and very often refiners sell a refined barrel of crude for less than it was bought. Increasingly, refiners are taking steps to protect their margins by employing hedging strategies rather than risk margin erosion due to commodity price volatility.

Physical Crude Oil Trading

Physical crude oil trading is the buying activity that refiners use to acquire raw crude feedstock for refineries. Refineries will buy crudes on the global market that meet their refining requirements. Integrated majors will not only refine their own equity crudes, they will also buy crudes on the global market when the economics are better. The majors may get better-refined margins buying cheaper crudes on the global market than refining their own crudes. Integrated majors may purchase crudes that are heavier and have higher sulfur content, because these crudes are less expensive than the lighter, sweeter crudes.

The integrated majors have world-class refineries with the units necessary to economically transform heavier crudes into diesel fuels and gasolines. These refineries are considered very complex and have cokers, hydrocrackers, and alkylation units necessary to transform heavier, sour crudes such as Mexican Maya into more valuable diesel fuels.

Refineries produce a variety of refined products with various grades of heating oil or distillates, jet fuel, gasoline, naphtha, residuals, and butanes. Often times, refiners can substitute one crude for another as long as it has similar crude characteristics. For example, North Sea Statjford may be substituted for Nigeria's Bonny Light. Both of these crudes are very light, sweet crudes with gravities in the range of 36°API. However, there may be occasions where Bonny Light is priced at a greater differential to Statjford. Crude oil supply is the other variable to be considered. Refiners and physical crude oil traders make daily decisions based on crude availability, price, transport cost, yield, and product quality.

A refinery's product slate, yield, geography, and season will determine which crudes are purchased. Refineries have complex computer models that determine the quantities, pricing, and numerous other optimization factors in buying crudes on the global market.

There is also a very distinct seasonality to gasoline and heating oil spot prices and futures contracts that trade on the global exchanges such as the New York Mercantile Exchange (NYMEX) or the Intercontinental Exchange (ICE) in London. This seasonality is driven by consumer demand for gasoline and diesel fuels in the northern hemisphere's summer driving season, primarily between May and September. Heating oil or gas oil demand increases with colder weather seasons. Refineries will ramp up production of both gasoline and heating oil products in anticipation of seasonal demands for both products. Refiner's traders will begin purchasing crudes for refinery feedstock supply considering all of these market parameters of supply and seasonal demands.

Refining Capacity, Complexity, and Utilization

Every refinery has a maximum capacity (or nameplate capacity) at which it can refine the barrels of raw crude into more valuable products, such as gasoline, heating oil, and jet fuel. Refineries can also be compared on a scale referred to as the Nelson Index. The Nelson Index allows comparisons of smaller, less complex refineries which might be able to process up to 30,000 to 60,000 barrels per day (bpd) with the complex refineries that can process in excess of 200,000 bpd of both sweet and sour crudes. In the United States, ExxonMobil's Baytown refinery in Texas along with BP's Texas City refinery are two of the largest and most complex refineries, each capable of refining more than 400,000 bpd of crude.

Refining complexity is measured by the Nelson Index, which ranks refineries on a scale between 2 and 12. The simplest refineries may not have hydrocrackers, cokers, or Alkylation Units. Complex refineries produce a variety of refined products and may have Alkylation Units or a hydrocracker used to produce alkylates, gasoline, or diesel fuels. Very complex refineries have the capacity to process heavy, sour crudes, and may have steam crackers for petrochemical products. Very complex refineries may also have gas treatment plants and cokers for heavier crudes.

FIGURE 9.1   EIA Refining Utilization Chart (%)

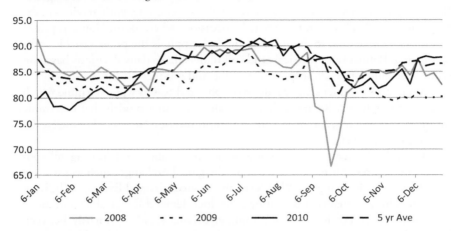

Source: U.S. Energy Information Administration (EIA).

Refining utilization, see Figure 9.1, is a measure of the percentage of total refining capacity actually being utilized at a given point in time. Recently, refining utilization has approximated 88 percent, reflecting modest recovery in both commercial and consumer demand. Emerging-market countries are posting refining utilizations in excess of 90 percent due to stronger economic growth.

Refining Margins

Refiners are in the economic dilemma of buying raw crudes, refining crudes, and then selling the refined products at a profit. In many cases, the profitability is negative, resulting in negative refined margins. Traders have the added complexity of incorporating transport costs into the crude buying equation. Transport costs play a significant role in the cost structure of buying and selling crudes. Crudes are typically transported via barges, tanker ships, or pipeline. Transport costs for each of these methods vary, in some cases daily, and will greatly influence the margins associated with purchasing and selling crudes and their refined products.

Regulatory costs, storage costs, working capital, and other internal operating costs also play a role in determining the refined margins. Refiners can influence their own internal cost structure, but have considerably less influence over other costs such as storage (unless it is their own) or transport—for example, pipeline or tanker ship.

Refined margins are also influenced by the base crude price, seasonality, and demand for refined products. Independent refiners are vulnerable to swings in commodity prices. It is imperative that they employ hedging strategies to mitigate the fluctuations in crude oil prices. Today, most independent refiners are actively utilizing risk management strategies to protect their margins. Some integrated majors are using the tools of futures to protect their margins. Many integrated majors are still fairly conservative in this arena.

Basic Terminology

There are more than 200 grades of crude worldwide. Each of these crudes varies by their density, viscosity, sulfur content, and numerous other specifications. This book wouldn't be complete if we didn't cover the very basics of these concepts—but it will be kept at a high level.

When crude oil is extracted from a given field, geological scientists and petroleum engineers will analyze a myriad of crude characteristics and specifications for a particular crude oil. Geologists and engineers will develop a laboratory analysis referred to in the industry as a *crude assay*. The crude assay is the road map providing viscosities, tan, sulfur content, pour points, and densities (and other attributes) at varying temperatures and pressures for a particular crude under a number of conditions. It is a complex document that provides buyers and sellers of crudes with essential information on a crude oil's specific characteristics. Most importantly, it guides refinery managers how best to refine and handle a particular crude oil. It is important to note that often times a crude oil's characteristics can vary within the same field.

Viscosity is a measure of crudes oil's ability to flow and is measured in centistokes. Viscosity is important, because crude oils are transported under varying temperatures, climates, and conditions.

The industry follows the guidelines devised by the API which has published guidelines on gravity and densities. Gravity measures a crude oil's density and is referred to in API degrees. The scale is an inverse scale, whereby crudes generally 36 degrees and above are considered light crudes. Crudes with APIs from 35 to 19 degrees are considered medium crudes. Crude oils with an API of 18 degrees and below are considered heavy crudes. Crude oil with an API less than 10 degrees would be considered ultra or extra heavy.

In general, heavier crudes are less desirable because they require additional refining requirements and this is reflected in their prices. Lighter, sweet crudes command higher prices on the global market. Benchmark crudes such as West Texas Intermediate (WTI) and Brent crudes are considered light, sweet crudes because their APIs are generally in the 36-degree range and they have low levels of sulfur. It is also worth mentioning that many refiners would prefer the more economical, heavier crudes provided that their refineries can process these crudes.

Sulfur content is a measure of the sulfur naturally found in all crudes. Generally, crudes that have less than 0.5 percent sulfur are generally deemed to be sweet crudes. Crudes that have greater than 2.0 percent are considered to be sour crudes. High sulfur content is not desirable for a number of reasons. Sulfur is a corrosive substance and various refining processes attempt to reduce sulfur content and improve viscosity levels.

Benchmark Crude Oils

What makes a benchmark crude oil? Why is it that the market turns to WTI and Brent crude as the benchmark crudes in the industry? In general, benchmark crudes should be highly liquid with market prices available 24/7. Crudes that do not trade daily are priced off of one of the benchmark crudes such as Brent, Dubai, WTI, Tapis, or Omani crudes.

In addition, benchmark crudes have ample production without concern of maturing basins. In recent years, crude oil production in the North Sea has been declining as it is a fairly mature basin. Over the years, the market has adapted by adopting other crudes with very similar characteristics in nearby basins such as Ekofisk, Forties, and Oseberg crudes as substitutes for Brent. Hence, the acronym BFOE Brent refers largely to North Sea crudes, all with very similar light, sweet crude characteristics. In this case, Forties and Ekofisk all have very similar crude characteristics. Today, the Brent Blend refers to a basket of North Sea crudes all with very similar crude characteristics.

Should Brent and WTI trade at the same price? Not necessarily. Brent crude prices reflect a very prolific North Sea commercial trade. WTI primarily reflects trade arriving in the Gulf of Mexico. Recently, the spread between Brent and WTI widened when the amount of oil stored in Cushing, Oklahoma, increased to levels near its maximum capacity. Historically, the spread between WTI and Brent daily spot or futures market prices has been in the plus or minus $2-per-barrel range. However, the Brent-WTI spread has recently widened to $15 per barrel as supplies increased in Cushing and Brent production has come under pressure. As previously mentioned, WTI may evolve into only a key North American benchmark crude price.

Crack Spreads

Crack spreads reflect the level of potential profitability generated by refiners for refining a barrel into its various refined products such as gasoline and heating oil. Refiners always prefer positive (and the higher, the better) crack spreads. Crack spreads are often negative, particularly when crude oil prices are very low near the $30- or $35-per-barrel mark as they were in the first quarter of 2009. Crack spreads were negative as economies went into recession and demand for crude products faltered. As global recovery improved, both refining margins and crack spreads rebounded.

3-2-1 Crack Spread

The 3-2-1 crack spread considers the theoretical profitability of refining three barrels of crude into one barrel of heating oil and two barrels of gasoline. Crack spreads are always measured in dollars per barrel. Heating oil and gasoline futures contracts trade in cents per gallon. Both contracts are, and have been, well above 100 cents per gallon. Therefore, we multiply the heating oil and gasoline prices by 42, because there are 42 gallons in a barrel. The formula is as follows:

$$3\text{-}2\text{-}1 = [(1 \times HO\ price \times 42) + (2 \times RBOB\ price \times 42) - (3 \times Crude\ Price)]/3$$

HO is the trading symbol for heating oil. RBOB is the trading symbol for Reformulated Blendstock for Oxygenate Blending base grade of gasoline. Both of these contracts trade on the NYMEX. This formula utilizes the closing price for both heating oil and RBOB. It is important to first have a view of the market. Refer to Figure 9.2 that illustrates the increase in the 3-2-1 crack spread as crude prices increased throughout 2010.

Refiners and energy traders are continuously analyzing the relationship between crude oil, gasoline, and heating oil to take advantage of opportunities in the market. If a refiner held the view that crude oil prices were going to remain robust and gasoline and diesel fuel prices were going to be lackluster or even fall, traders may enter into a single order by simultaneously purchasing the crude oil futures and selling the gasoline and heating oil futures contract or "selling the crack."

Conversely, traders can "buy the crack" by executing the reverse: Selling crude oil futures and buying futures contracts for the refined products of

FIGURE 9.2   3-2-1 Crack spread ($ per barrel)

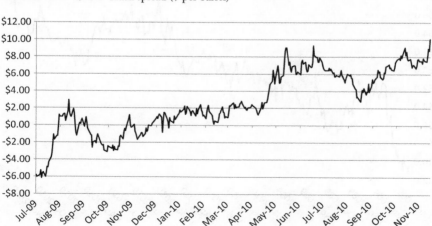

Source: Bloomberg.

gasoline or diesel fuel. Refiners are usually in this position, because they are always buying crudes and selling their refined products. Refiners will either "buy or sell" the crack spread depending on their inventory levels, cash markets, and contractual needs.

It is important to note that a 3:2:1 crack spread is widely used in the North American market. However, European markets or other geographies that use considerable amounts of diesel fuel instead of gasoline, may opt for other variations on the crack spread such as a 5:3:2 crack spread. In North America, gasoline is used more prevalently than diesel and hence, in the equation, gasoline is multiplied by two for two barrels. Crack spreads are flexible and meant to reflect the slate of products that a given refinery produces for its market.

Heat and Gas Crack

Analysts often calculate crack spreads on the refined products known as the Heat Crack and Gas Crack, which measures the profitability of producing gasoline or diesel fuel from crude oil. Both of these crack spreads are measured in dollars per barrel. Refer to Figure 9.3 that depicts the Gasoline Crack Spread throughout the latter half of 2009 and most of 2010. As one might expect, seasonality plays a definite role as demand for heating oil increases in the winter months, so heating oil prices increase. Northern hemisphere winters play a considerable role

FIGURE 9.3   Gasoline Crack spread ($ per barrel)

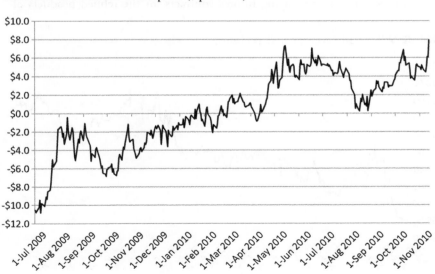

Source: Bloomberg.

by increasing the demand for heating oil which results in increasing the heat crack spread.

$$\text{Heat Crack} = 42 \times (\text{Heating oil price}) - \text{Crude oil price}$$

$$\text{Gasoline Crack} = 42 \times (\text{RBOB price}) - \text{Crude oil price}$$

RBOB can be substituted with any other gasoline price such as CBOB (California Reformulated Blendstock for Oxygenate Blending). The concept is to evaluate the theoretical profitability of producing gasoline. Like heating oil, the gasoline crack spread is influenced by seasonal supply and demand for gasoline. A robust northern hemisphere summer driving season often leads to increases in the gasoline crack spread. Refiners will enter into hedges by buying or selling the heat crack or gas crack to preserve their profit margin month by month.

Traders and refiners are keenly aware of how prices around the globe in the cash market are moving relative to that of the futures market. These relationships are complex and often provide opportunity to manage risk by hedging.

The Challenge

Most refiners purchase raw crudes on the global market approximately 20 to 30 days in advance of their refining schedules. Integrated majors will refine much of their own crudes and purchase crudes on the open market. Few refineries ever have a full slate of all crudes that are necessary to produce the products they desire. Therein lays the challenge. Refineries purchase crudes at market prices to refine into varying grades of gasoline and diesel fuel. Refiners are essentially on both sides of the fence. The other side of this equation is the fact that once a barrel of crude is refined into gasoline or diesel, it gets sold to a refiner's contractual clients. This can be a recipe for economic trouble if a barrel of product gets sold for less than what the refinery paid for the raw crude.

Outlook

The impact of the 2008 to 2009 recessionary environment and downturn in refined products demand has resulted in an increase in refinery closures. In both the United States and Europe, refinery closures have made headlines heralding the end of an era of robust demand for gasoline and distillate products. The most notable closure was that of the Dunkirk refinery in France where workers staged repeated strikes in an effort to get Total's management to agree to not close additional refineries in the Total refining system. This is but one example of numerous European and U.S. refinery closures or conversions to terminals or petrochemical plants.

Even though Organization for Economic Cooperation and Development (OECD) economies are in the midst of a modest economic recovery, we are witness to one of the most significant retrenchments in decades. Refiners around the globe are shedding unprofitable assets. We will continue to see consolidation among smaller refiners in efforts to gain economies of scale.

In the current environment, refinery closures are becoming commonplace in OECD countries. In emerging market countries, they need refining capacity and are pushing the limits of existing refining assets. Countries such as Brazil, Saudi Arabia, and certain Asian economies already have new refineries on the drawing board. Their current refining utilization rate is in the lower 90 percent range.

Among U.S. and European economies, refinery modification and upgrades are more common in the current economic environment. Simple refineries are beginning to add on units such as cokers that will enable them to purchase and refine heavier, higher sulfur crudes. The capital expenditure of upgrading units is still significant. This reflects the increased demand for higher sulfur heavier crudes which will continue amid a modest, but growing recovery.

Concluding Thoughts

As crude oil prices have rebounded, the 3-2-1 crack spread is currently near an unprecedented $25 per barrel as crude oil prices surge. Throughout 2011, the crack spread environment has been very supportive, reflecting positive crack spreads most of 2010 and into 2011. Many independent refiners have posted increases in quarterly earnings on the heels of higher crude prices and increased demand for crude and refined products. Improvements in the global economy are certainly benefitting the refiners. At the same time, integrated majors are increasingly taking the position to rationalize refining assets. The refining industry is still not operating at pre-2008 levels. Therefore, we expect continued divestitures of unprofitable refining assets around the globe.

CHAPTER 10

Integrated Majors and the Evolution of the Competitive Landscape

The global crude oil industry has undergone significant changes over the last three decades. Within the industry, numerous technological developments have taken place as exploration and oil and gas drilling have remarkably advanced beyond expectations. Profound developments within the technological arena abound as producers continually push scientific, geological, and engineering capabilities to new levels. What does that translate into for the consumer, producer, and commercial users of refined products?

In addition, the competitive arena has changed for integrated majors as they now face two very significant challenges: Growing the reserve base and increasing production. There is no doubt that geopolitics are forces to be reckoned with in the global oil and gas industry. What also remains is the working relationship between the integrated majors or independent oil companies (IOCs) and those that are state-owned or national oil companies (NOCs). The working relationships have evolved and reflect the existing economic environment at any given time.

Role of National Oil Companies

Indeed, the tables have turned for some NOCs. During the financial crisis of 2008 to 2009, many NOCs found themselves in a disturbing predicament where they needed funding, technology, and resources that many IOCs accumulated during the bull run years of crude oil prices from 2006 to mid-2008. For some NOCs this situation has not improved while other NOCs have emerged relatively unscathed.

Today, IOCs are challenged to explore and develop reserves in the frontier of the oil and gas industry. The era of easy oil is undeniably over. What does that mean for producers? Producers are challenged to explore for hydrocarbons in ultra deep waters, the Arctic Circle, unconventional natural gas shales, and some of the most geologically challenging locations on the planet in order to maintain the crude oil and natural gas production status quo and grow their reserve base.

Resource Nationalization

One of the most significant challenges for IOCs is access to reserves. Now more than ever, natural resources have certainly become a strategic advantage for sovereign nations. Increasingly, IOCs have to work with NOCs as Organization of Petroleum Exporting Countries (OPEC) own nearly 79 percent of reserves according to the *BP Statistical Review of World Energy June 2010*. The mineral and natural resource laws in other countries simply do not provide for IOCs to develop oil and gas reserves. NOCs have claimed natural reserves as their own if found in their country. To the extent NOCs have progressive oil and gas regulatory regimes, IOCs may consider participation with these countries. Some NOCs are implementing regulatory regimes making it unattractive for IOCs. Examples of such countries are Bolivia, Venezuela, and Ecuador. Each of these countries has instituted certain levels of resource nationalization. All three countries have actually nationalized assets belonging to IOCs who were working in basins on major projects.

The result is that IOCs eventually seek to leave these countries. In 2007, the most extreme case is the situation where ExxonMobil's production was halted along with other IOCs in Venezuela's Orinoco Belt. What began as a partnership deteriorated into legal action when Venezuela's Hugo Chavez declared that Petróleos de Venezuela S.A. (PDVSA) would automatically own 60 percent of all crude oil production by implementing his *Empresas Mixtas* policy. A few companies decided to stay and renegotiate their contracts with PDVSA while other IOCs left Venezuela. ExxonMobil and PDVSA ended up in international arbitration in The Hague. This will no doubt take years of legal proceedings to sort itself out. This situation illustrated the level of vulnerability of many IOCs operating in countries that have a significant change in energy policy.

Both Ecuador and Bolivia instituted similar policies between 2006 and 2008. The net effect of nationalization is essentially to drive out foreign investment. Bolivia has paid a high price for such policies. While Bolivia can lay claim to 16 tcf of natural gas reserves, Bolivia is challenged to extract and develop its natural gas reserves. The result was natural gas shortages to neighboring Argentina in 2006 to 2008 that adversely impacted other South American countries.

The laws of each country are very different. What is common among many nations is that the state owns the mineral rights. Few countries are the exception to this practice. In Chapter 14, we will examine the peculiarities of countries that have what is referred to as NOCs with hybrid structures or mixed-capital companies. These countries have yet another business model that is much more progressive and business friendly.

The Road Ahead for Integrated Majors

In an environment of mid to lower crude oil prices, integrated majors or IOCs find themselves in greater demand. As crude oil prices decline, NOCs will encounter greater economic pressures and home economies bear the brunt of decreased oil revenue. Conversely, IOCs do not have the financial pressures of supporting sovereigns and repatriating cash flows to home governments. Most IOCs have considerable resources, in terms of both technology and financial wherewithal, to withstand economic shocks of declining crude oil prices. As a result, IOCs are increasingly in demand as joint venture partners. While the landscape for IOCs may appear ominous, IOCs certainly have a future as increased demand for energy places IOCs in a position to capitalize on future demand growth.

It is important to note that not all NOCs are created equal. While reserves matter, so do regulatory regimes. NOCs with more progressive regulatory environments will be better able to take advantage of increased energy demand over the next two decades. Why? These NOCs will have the flexibility to react and take advantage of opportunities. The best examples of NOCs with progressive regulatory regimes are Norway's Statoil Hydro and Brazil's Petróleo Brasileiro S.A. (Petrobras). These two NOCs have adopted many of the best practices of IOCs. Statoil Hydro and Petrobras are both very competitive and operate in countries with democracies and laws protecting contract sanctity. As a result, IOCs are eager to work with these companies.

U.S. Safety and Regulation

There is no doubt that drilling safety is of considerable importance to oil and gas producers, regulators, and the public at large. In many countries, increased regulation has now become an integral part of the offshore drilling industry. In addition, there are new levels of complexity and uncertainly associated with offshore drilling, particularly in the United States. As a result of the April 2010 Deepwater Horizon oil spill in the U.S. Gulf of Mexico, the former U.S. Bureau of Minerals Management Service was restructured and became the Bureau of Ocean Energy Management, Regulation, and Enforcement (BOEMRE) under the auspices of the U.S. Department of the Interior.

Since the April 2010 disaster, BOEMRE developed increased safety measures for energy development on the Outer Continental Shelf (OCS) to prevent such a disaster from recurring. First and foremost among producers is a general certification of compliance with existing regulations and national safety alert. According to BOEMRE, operators must attest to numerous safety measures including the following.

- Examination of all well-control system equipment (both surface and subsea) currently being used to ensure that is has been properly maintained and is capable of shutting down the well during emergency operations. Ensure blowout preventers (BOPs) are able to perform their designated functions.
- Review all rig drilling, casing, cementing, well abandonment (temporary and permanent), completion, and workover practices to ensure that well control is not compromised at any point while the BOP is installed on the wellhead.
- Review all emergency shutdown and dynamic positioning procedures that interface with emergency well-control operations.
- Ensure that all personnel involved in well operations are properly trained and capable of performing their tasks under both normal drilling and emergency well-control operations.

In addition, operators must have their chief executive officers attest that they are in compliance with each of the above requirements. According to BOEMRE, false statements are considered a criminal offense. There are numerous other requirements specifically addressing the BOP, its configuration, performance, well-control systems, inspections, maintenance, repairs, subsea BOP stacks, well design, and construction of wells. The BOEMRE further states that failure to certify all requirements "will result in the issuance of an incident of non-compliance and may result in a shut-in order." There is no doubt there is renewed emphasis by U.S. regulators on safety and standards compliance.

As the industry complies and institutes its own set of safety compliance criteria, I anticipate that offshore drilling in the United States will undoubtedly slow down. The oil and gas industry has moved to institute better emergency response plans, most notably cooperative initiatives among several integrated majors led by ExxonMobil. Improvements in emergency response will continue to unfold throughout the industry. In addition, I expect cost structures among global integrated majors to increase as they seek to meet new U.S. regulatory and safety criteria.

UK Environmental Program

Integrated majors are also moving to comply with increased environmental regulation around the globe. Many countries have instituted new environmental offshore drilling requirements and development regulations. As integrated majors seek to participate in bid rounds, environmental laws and regulations will increasingly play a role in various markets.

The UK's Strategic Environmental Assessment (SEA) procedures works in conjunction with the UK Department of Energy and Climate Change (DECC) to identify which blocks can participate in oil and gas licensing rounds in keeping with environmental concerns. According to DECC (www.offshore-sea.org.uk), "DECC has taken a proactive stance on the use of SEA as a means of striking a balance between promoting economic development of the UK's offshore energy resources and effective environmental protection." For the 26th Seaward Licensing Round, the SEA report identified certain blocks in the UK Continental Shelf such as 10 blocks in the Moray Firth and 11 blocks in the Cardigan Bay area to be withheld from the licensing round. The SEA report identifies the impact on protected conservation sites. As a result, certain blocks may be withheld from bid rounds subject to further review and information collection. The SEA reports are living documents that will evolve over time.

The DECC subdivided the UK Continental Shelf into eight geographic areas along the English, Welsh, Scottish, and Irish coastlines and the English Channel. Drilling in the nearby North Sea has been ongoing for almost the last 50 years, by many United Kingdom producers and other integrated majors. The SEA program brings together industry experts, conservation experts, and governmental authorities. The SEA program will evolve and be refined as the process continues. What this illustrates is the extent to which the licensing and permitting process will be a lengthy investment of time and resources by the integrated majors as environmental concerns increase in many markets.

Technological Challenges Abound

The integrated majors will continue to be at the forefront of technology when compared to some of their NOC counterparts. The competitive landscape will be marked by those companies that have developed technical expertise, as it will become a key competitive advantage. Whether it be deepwater drilling, unconventional shale expertise, or exploring in the Arctic Circle, those majors with technological expertise will prevail and become the most sought-after project partners. There have been numerous technological advancements in the last 20 years in the oil and gas industry such as directional drilling, seismic technology, and satellite technology. Many of these technologies have helped to reduce the overall cost of crude on a per-barrel basis.

Directional Drilling

Over the last decade, the oil and gas industry has widely incorporated the advent of horizontal drilling over drilling vertically. Producers no longer drill only vertically, but have increased flexibility with drilling direction. The primary benefit of horizontal drilling is the ability to drill into multiple horizontal reservoirs through one well. Many reservoirs are physically situated such that a drill bit can be maneuvered to reach multiple reservoirs. In addition, producers have the ability to drill for miles to the oil or gas source.

The economic benefit is considerable. The environmental footprint reduction is considerable as there are fewer drill rigs to construct. Equally important are the potential increases in production as one drilling system is able to extract hydrocarbons from numerous reservoirs. Production increases with directional drilling systems are estimated to be ten times that of conventional drilling systems. As a result, over the last several years, horizontal drilling has become very prevalent in the industry.

Seismic Surveys

The development of three-dimensional (3-D) seismic testing has enabled the oil and gas industry to peer into what might otherwise be hidden geologic structures. Using 3D seismic testing enables geological teams to model all aspects of geological structures to determine whether the hydrocarbon potential is worth pursuing. One must bear in mind that geological structures (or traps as they are known) vary. Basins are identified by both their geologic age and geologic structure. Geologic age is identified by the age of the basin and the depth of the rock layers. Layers are identified by their age, such as Mesozoic, Paleozoic, Jurassic periods, and so on.

Seismic surveys utilize sound waves to develop images of subsurface strata and determine where hydrocarbons might be present. Seismic survey vessels emit sound waves which bounce off of subsea rock formations. These reflected sound waves are captured by hydrophone steamers and the collected data is later analyzed by computers in 3D imagery. The 3D geologic evaluations and imagery help guide scientists to determine whether to pursue further testing or drill so-called appraisal wells if recoverable hydrocarbons appear to be present.

Enhanced Oil Recovery

Every crude oil or natural gas basin has a life production span. Integrated majors are challenged to manage the natural decline of a field within a basin. As such, integrated majors or oil service companies are often utilizing enhanced oil-recovery systems used to breathe new life into mature or declining oil wells. The enhanced oil-recovery system utilizes injecting various fluids or natural gas into a field to create upward pressure on the hydrocarbons toward a well bore. According to ExxonMobil (www.exxonmobil.com), oil or gas recovery can increase up to three fold. Expertise in these systems is becoming a competitive advantage as existing fields mature.

Unconventional Natural Gas Shales

In the last few years, newer discoveries of unconventional natural gas shales have the potential to double U.S. natural gas reserves from 300 to upward of 600 tcf. The United States and Canada have some of the most prolific natural gas reserves, which many in the North American oil and gas industry are now vying to obtain. In addition, European and Asian oil and gas producers are actively acquiring acreage in North America to obtain access to natural gas shale formations in various plays throughout the United States and Canada.

The increase in unconventional natural gas reserves has the potential to provide natural gas supplies to North America for a decade or more. Just as producers jockey for acreage, regulators are still determining whether hydraulic fracturing is potentially harmful to drinking water.

In the natural gas arena, hydraulic fracturing is a development that is pushing the frontier of natural gas development. Conventional natural gas production takes place with a traditional drill rig and Christmas tree (the set of valves and fittings connected to the top of the well) configuration. However, spurred by the discovery of unconventional natural gas shales, hydraulic fracturing utilizes high water pressure to break up dense shale rock in order to release the hydrocarbons that are buried deep within this rock.

Reserve Changes

In 2008, the Securities and Exchange Commission (SEC) revised regulations and definitions of what can be considered proven reserves. This is a very significant and long-awaited win for the industry. The SEC finally recognized that technological changes in the industry need to be acknowledged and original standards by which proven reserves were measured are indeed antiquated. Previously, definitions of crude reserves were established in the 1930s. Oil and gas technology has come a long way, making existing reserve definitions dated. While all producers who sell securities in the United States abide by the SEC definition of proven reserves and regulations for its disclosure, the change in the definition to a more liberal definition opens the door to a re-evaluation of proven reserves.

Presently, the SEC stipulates that so-called proven reserves have to be deemed commercially viable by both fairly complex scientific and geological testing. There are a handful of firms in the world today that certify such reserves. The SEC is finally recognizing that technology has indeed changed from original rules established in the 1930s. Today, global oil and gas producers are extracting methane from coal beds and exploiting unconventional natural gas reserves once thought impossible to access. The use of horizontal drilling is prevalent in the industry and has become accepted standard practice. Such drilling technology did not exist when SEC proven reserve definitions were originally written.

Concluding Thoughts

Over the next several years, integrated majors will face increasing challenges not only from NOCs, but smaller exploration and production (E&P)-focused firms. There are numerous smaller, independent companies that aren't saddled with refineries or retail gasoline stations that are nimble and able to react to opportunities in the market. Many of these smaller firms have increasingly strong balance sheets and are able to access capital with similar ease to that of many majors. This new cadre of competitors will provide integrated majors considerable competition or present possible partnership or acquisition opportunities.

CHAPTER 11

The Oilfield Service Sector and Oil Juniors

This chapter examines two very important oil and gas industry players: the service sector companies and oil juniors. The oilfield service sector consists of both larger and smaller companies hired by the majors to drill wells and provide highly specialized drill-rig services at the specification of the operators. In the aftermath of the 2010 Gulf of Mexico disaster, this working relationship has come under intense scrutiny by politicians and regulators.

We also review the growing role that oil juniors play in the industry. Oil juniors are small- and mid-cap companies whose only focus is exploration and production (E&P). These companies are not exposed to the vagaries of downstream operations such as refining, transport, storage, and retail operations. Not only do they have smaller capital structures, but they are highly specialized in their E&P work. Oil juniors are increasingly leading the way on certain projects in more liberalized regulatory frameworks.

The World Is Their Platform

In a post Macondo world, the oil industry will never be the same. The service companies and operators are in a new world order with, perhaps, a new playbook. What the 2010 Gulf of Mexico oil spill illustrated was the complexity with which operators and service companies must work together. The traditional model has come under scrutiny and is open to a new business model with renewed focus on safety and planning for the unthinkable. Increased governmental regulation will necessitate a thorough review of existing operational and safety practices.

The oil field service sector often warrants some of the glory that is associated with announcements by the operators of major crude or natural gas discoveries. In the oil and gas industry, operators and the service sector are inextricably linked not only operationally, but economically. Drill rig activity is a constant indicator of growth in the industry. It is an indicator of which geographies are actively in a production mode and similarly which are retrenching.

Technology Breaks New Frontiers

The global oil and gas producing industry is continually breaking new ground with announcements of oil discoveries that are increasingly deeper within the Earth's crust or beneath the oceans' surface. We begin in 2007 with Petrobras's announcement of its deepwater discovery in the South Atlantic, approximately two miles beneath the ocean's surface and another three to four miles below the sea floor into massive layers of salt deposits. Petrobras has established itself as a producer with a considerable level of deepwater drilling expertise. In 2009, BP announced its Tiber discovery in the U.S. Gulf of Mexico. The Tiber discovery is in 4,132 feet (1,259 meters) of water with a well that has been drilled 35,055 feet (10,685 meters)—one of the deepest in the industry. This discovery is in an area once thought to be dormant and abandoned by the majors. In 2010, the New Orleans-based team McMoRan marked a major discovery at the Davey Jones basin, also in the Gulf of Mexico. This natural gas discovery will require a drilling depth of approximately 28,000 feet.

What is the future of deepwater drilling? Despite the 2010 Gulf of Mexico oil spill, the industry is proceeding with deepwater exploration and projects around the globe. In the wake of the Gulf of Mexico oil spill, the U.S. government temporarily banned deepwater drilling. In the United States, deepwater drilling officially resumed in October 2010, but as regulators are increasing safety requirements among operators, few permits have been issued. However, in other countries, deepwater drilling is moving full speed ahead. During the U.S. moratorium, a small number of deepwater drill rigs left the United States for other geographies friendlier to deepwater drilling.

Economics of the Oilfield Service Sector: Feast or Famine

Like the rest of the oil and gas industry, the oil field service sector is highly vulnerable to volatility in crude oil prices. Typically, oil field service companies enter into long-term contracts with oil and gas operators to supply the necessary drill rigs, semi submersibles, and other drilling equipment. The demand for drilling equipment mirrors demand for crude products. In a high crude oil price environment, operators are eager to extract every barrel, and demand for drill rigs escalates. The standard practice in the industry is for oilfield service companies to charge day rates. The result is day rates for drill rigs, semis, and similar equipment that can quickly skyrocket as they did in 2007 and early 2008. When crude oil prices reached $147 per barrel, service companies could select projects and

FIGURE 11.1 Baker Hughes Worldwide Drill Rig Count

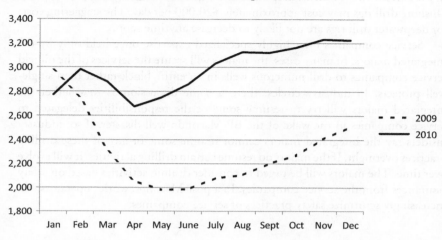

Source: Baker Hughes.

operators virtually on their terms. Demand for services far outpaced the supply of rigs. Similarly, when crude oil prices collapsed as they did in the fourth quarter of 2008, day rates came under pressure. What about those long-term contractual arrangements? Invariably, operators try to get oil field service companies back to the negotiating table to re-negotiate contracts reflecting a new price environment. Figure 11.1 is the Baker Hughes Drill Rig Chart, which illustrates the correlation between commodity prices and drilling activity.

Texas-based Baker Hughes, a leading global oil field service sector company, provides the industry a tremendous service by tracking global drill rig activity. This is an excellent barometer for industry activity for both natural gas and crude oil drilling all over the globe.

Equipment Backlog

The service sector secures projects years in advance. Their contracts are long term and pricing reflects the current demand for crude oil. One of the most important metrics is the order backlog for service companies. Currently, the industry is moving at a good pace, with new orders coming online. During the financial crisis, higher-risk projects were placed on the backburner by operators, resulting in many layoffs at service companies. By 2011, many projects were resumed and day-rate pricing has remained relatively firm.

Onshore drilling costs remain considerably more economical than that of offshore. Similarly, shallow water drill rigs are more economical than deepwater.

In the current environment, deepwater drill rigs can cost up to $500,000 per day. Onshore drill rigs may cost approximately $20,000 per day. The staggering costs for deepwater drill rigs are not likely to decrease anytime soon.

Service companies offer highly specialized expertise once held only by the integrated majors. In many cases, the majors will secure the services of the oilfield service companies to drill numerous wells in an entire block rather than single-well projects. In industry circles, there is some discussion as to whether the integrated majors will try to resume some of the responsibilities delegated to service companies in the wake of the BP Macondo well disaster. If so, industry insiders say the integrated majors cannot resume some or any of these drilling practices overnight. If the majors do resume certain drilling activities, it will evolve over time. The majors will be urged to consider drilling activities based on safety assurances from the service companies. In a post-Macondo world, operators will increasingly scrutinize safety practices of service companies.

The Outlook

As a result of the Gulf of Mexico disaster, the relationship between producers and oil field service companies will be indelibly changed. The legal aspects are most notable, in that operators will continue to try to ensure service companies absorb as much of the risk as possible.

Going forward, expect operators to more closely scrutinize working relationships with service companies. In addition, there will be consolidation in the service sector industry. Smaller service companies with weaker balance sheets will not be able to withstand the potential liability associated with the riskier projects such as deepwater drilling.

Oil Juniors: Is Smaller Better?

Oil juniors play an increasingly important role in global exploration and production. Oil juniors are not weighed down by the pricing risks of refining operations or a gasoline retail network with paper-thin margins. Oil juniors are lean machines, the hired guns of the oil industry with specific drilling expertise in hard-to-reach locales often shunned by the majors. The result is a cadre of exciting stories of investment, growth, and, yes, failure that often precedes success. The following is a list of criteria that we find critical to success among oil juniors.

Experience Is Everything

The most successful oil juniors are often comprised of very experienced management teams. In this industry, there is no substitute for experience. Many of the senior managers at oil juniors were recruited from the integrated majors. These management teams bring agility, technical expertise, and knowledge of certain blocks critical to early success. Typically, oil juniors begin life as a micro-cap firm where funding is critical to early exploration and development activities.

Along with success comes failure. Many oil juniors have a track record of success delivered by the management team. However, equally important are the well and drilling failures and the learning associated with those experiences. Failure makes for critical geological and engineering learning opportunities.

Capitalization Is Critical

One cannot overemphasize the importance of adequate capitalization. Oil juniors are particularly susceptible to market downturns. During the financial crisis of 2008 to 2009, many oil juniors had to idle drill rigs while waiting for crude oil prices to return to more palatable levels. The challenge is managing the volatility of the commodity cycle. At crude oil prices of $35 per barrel, production is often not feasible for micro-cap firms. In a capital intensive industry, micro-cap firms must have adequate financial reserves in order to withstand a market downturn.

Debt versus Equity

For micro- and small-cap firms, the challenge is access to capital. Is equity financing more desirable than debt financing? Which is more accessible? Currently, credit financing has retrenched and is not available the way it was prior to 2008. Bank financing dried up for many of these smaller firms. The market situation leaves bond financing and equity issuances. These alternatives are equally challenging for micro- and small-cap firms.

Public debt issuances require a rating from one of the rating agencies. This may or may not be desirable for micro- and small-cap firms. The cost, pricing, and market acceptance will drive whether this is a feasible option. Small- and micro-cap firms must ask if there is investor appetite for small-cap risk. Certainly, pricing will dictate whether this option is economically palatable. Any investor will require thorough due diligence. Oil juniors should be working with the appropriate advisors in order to navigate securities laws in the respective jurisdiction of issuance.

Of critical importance is the financial health of the company. Is the oil junior constrained or burdened by existing debt? What is the proforma impact of a new debt issuance? Potential investors and the management team should assess the financial impact of a new debt issuance.

In this industry, scale and jurisdiction are important. Smaller firms will be compared to industry peers, many of whom will have more financial and operational resources. As an example, if a firm issues a bond in a country whose sovereign rating is a B+/Stable Outlook, the firm may be capped by the B+ rating of the sovereign. The sovereign rating is very important and will often act as a ceiling for corporate ratings. There may be some flexibility, plus or minus a notch, depending on the circumstances. Most rating agencies will cap ratings by the rating of sovereign. This practice may have a very adverse affect on a potential issuer. Jurisdiction greatly matters.

A private debt issuance may have more appeal for small- and micro-cap firms. Private investors with whom one can have a meaningful dialogue could be more appealing. A private issuance also requires the appropriate advisors and investors that will conduct thorough due diligence. More important, debt issuances will necessitate the ability to fund debt service through cash flow. Oil juniors must be generating sufficient cash flow in order to pursue public or private debt issuances.

Equity Issuances

Are equity issuances the holy grail? For many oil juniors, it is the moment of truth. At what stage should an oil junior pursue the equity markets? Which equity market holds the most opportunity? There are numerous considerations that must be evaluated.

There is a track record of numerous success stories from smaller firms that have completed successful initial public offerings on the Toronto Stock Exchange (TSX) and the London Stock Exchange's AIM platform. Both of these exchanges are small-company friendly and understand the growing pains associated with micro- and small-cap oil companies. Oil juniors must be at a point in their life cycle where taking on the discipline and regulatory requirements of a major exchange are part and parcel of their everyday operation.

Making the leap to public company status is no small feat. Investors should look for oil juniors with the appropriate legal and financial infrastructure. These smaller firms must have the capability to issue accurate quarterly and annual financial statements without interruption. Oil juniors must have an investor relations staff at the ready to tell their story to global investors with conviction and understanding of the industry complexities. In addition, the legal requirements of securities law compliance represent additional overhead considerations. Oil juniors must have the legal support necessary to meet regulatory requirements of their jurisdiction and exchange.

There are numerous success stories in this arena. Over the last several years, many oil juniors have had successful equity issuances. What are the keys to success? These firms have management teams with a track record. These teams have a history of success and failure critical in this industry. These small- and micro-cap firms have built operational and financial infrastructure to meet the rigors of a public company. Small- and micro-cap firms operate in business-friendly countries with regulatory frameworks conducive to success. There will be more on this in later pages.

Regulatory Frameworks

The most successful oil juniors operate in countries that are small-company friendly. Not every jurisdiction is small-company friendly. In addition, successful oil juniors operate in countries that have the most liberal oil frameworks permitting entry of foreign corporations. Some of the best examples of countries that meet this criterion are Colombia and Peru. Both of these countries have some of the most progressive oil laws in the industry. Both countries welcome small-company participation and have structured their laws to attract foreign investment. This type of regulatory framework enables oil juniors to build up financial and operational resources and continue investing with the least amount of regulatory and geopolitical risk.

Operational Excellence

Oil juniors have a cadre of local expertise critical to successful drilling. Many of the most successful oil juniors hire locally and have built successful partnerships with local governmental authorities and regulators. This is critical to early planning and long-term success in a given country. Successful oil junior have also built operational teams with specific knowledge of blocks with critical engineering and seismic data. These teams are imperative to well successes and build important relationships with jurisdiction regulators.

Case Study: Gran Tierra Energy Inc.

One of the most successful oil juniors is that of Gran Tierra (AMEX:GTE) a Calgary-based publicly held company. In 2005, Gran Tierra began operations as a small eight-person firm dedicated to oil and gas exploration and development in Colombia, Peru, and Argentina.

Gran Tierra is an example of what can be achieved, in this case, in the equity markets. Gran Tierra chose the public equity markets as their vehicle to increase funding without jeopardizing the balance sheet. In 2006, Gran Tierra made its initial public offering. Since then, the company has gone to the capital markets on two other occasions, in 2008 and again in 2010. Gran Tierra was able to raise the needed funds to expand and grow its capital expenditure and acquisition program without adding debt to its balance sheet.

What was apparent is that this company assembled a team of knowledgeable experts throughout its organization. The Gran Tierra team knew drilling, but they quickly brought together a team of locals who helped navigate the regulatory process and build credibility in local markets.

The real estate slogan of location, location, and location is equally applicable in matters of oil geology. Gran Tierra chose Colombia and Peru as their primary markets in which to explore for and develop hydrocarbons. Colombia and

Peru have two of the most progressive energy frameworks in Latin America. Both geology and location matter indeed.

This strategy has paid dividends both literally and figuratively for Gran Tierra. As a result, Colombia and Peru have approximately 75 concessions each operating in their countries. In the industry, both countries are known for being small-company friendly. Both countries actively solicit business investment from outside Latin America.

In 2006, Gran Tierra's proven reserves were 600,000 barrels of oil equivalent. According to company data, at the end of fiscal 2009 proven oil reserves were an amazing 19.2 million barrels of oil equivalent across numerous basins in Peru, Colombia, and Argentina. In the same time frame, Gran Tierra has grown annual production from 300,000 barrels in 2006 to 4.6 million barrels in 2009. Gran Tierra is a remarkable story of a very successful oil junior and that is accomplishing big things.

Concluding Thoughts

Both oil juniors and oilfield service sector companies are critical players in the oil industry. The working relationship between the oilfield service sector and operators has come under intense scrutiny by regulators all over the globe. In a post Macondo world, operators will now re-assess the service sector in terms of enhanced safety measures, technological capabilities, and their emergency response.

Look to oil juniors for investment opportunities. This cadre of companies is on the exploration and production forefront in many emerging markets, particularly Latin America. There are numerous oil juniors that have found the Promised Land in markets such as Columbia and Peru.

CHAPTER 12

OPEC

In this chapter we review key aspects of the Organization of Petroleum Exporting Countries (OPEC), its pricing practices, some historical aspects, and its role during the downturn of the commodity cycle of 2008 to 2009. OPEC was organized by five oil-producing member countries on September 1, 1960, in Baghdad, Iraq. Its founding members are Saudi Arabia, Venezuela, Iran, Iraq, and Kuwait. OPEC today is a cartel consisting of 12 oil-producing countries. Its headquarters is in Vienna, Austria, and the group generally holds quarterly meetings to discuss global crude prices and crude production quotas for its members.

OPEC Organization

OPEC has established what is known as quotas whereby each member country abides by production guidelines. Technically, these are not published production guidelines, but rather an assessment of each country's general allocation of total crude production. The group does publically announce whether it will increase or decrease production and its intended production target. This is known as the Call on OPEC. OPEC will also provide its view of crude prices and its intentions, generally through its secretary general and its membership. In recent years, OPEC has become media savvy and various members have held news conferences and given brief interviews.

OPEC's secretary general is designated for a three-year term. It is an appointed position, nominated by the OPEC conference. Today, OPEC has a total of 12 members including Iraq. OPEC-11 is how the 12 members excluding Iraq are known. Each of the 11 members will generally follow its production guidelines or quotas. Iraq does not have any production quotas as it is rebuilding its oil-producing infrastructure that has been damaged by years of war and mismanagement.

Ecuador and Angola are OPEC's newest members, both having joined in 2007. This is Ecuador's second tour of duty with OPEC, as it suspended its membership in 1992 only to rejoin in 2007. Ecuador originally joined OPEC in 1973 when its oil producing capabilities were just beginning to develop. One can argue whether OPEC membership has actually helped or hindered a country like Ecuador. As an OPEC member, it must abide by the production guidelines and simply must produce crude at its production quota. Therein lays the challenge for each of OPEC's members. In 2009, Indonesia resigned its OPEC membership. There is more on production dilemmas later.

OPEC can and does accept new members to its ranks—albeit those countries who are invited. OPEC publishes by-laws stating its membership articles and requirements. Over the years, OPEC has tried to sway Russia, Norway, and a few other countries to join. OPEC membership is not for every country.

Angola is one of the newer members to meet its membership requirements. According to OPEC's 2008 Statues, Chapter II, Article 7, section C states, "any other country with a substantial net export of crude petroleum, which has fundamentally similar interest to those of Member countries, may become a Full Member of the Organization, if accepted by a majority of three-fourths of Full Members, including concurrent vote of all Founder Members."

Over the years, OPEC has tried to recruit new members. More than a decade ago, Norway, Russia, and Mexico were frequent participants at OPEC meetings because of their importance to global markets. Ten to 15 years ago, Mexico and Norway were in peak production years and had a great deal of influence. While Norway and Mexico are still considerable producers, Mexico's crude production is waning with the natural decline of its Cantarell basin in the Gulf of Mexico. Similarly, Norway has its own issues with the natural decline of the North Seas basins most notably Brent crude and other similar lighter crude oils.

OPEC Crude Basket

The new OPEC crude basket consists of 12 crudes from each of its producing members. Table 12.1 lists OPEC members and their respective OPEC reference crude basket. Some of these crudes are in high demand, because of their charac-teristics. Crudes such as Nigeria's Bonny Light continue to be sought after because it is considered a light, sweet crude. Similarly, Girassol produced by Angola is a desirable crude. Venezuela's crudes tend to be on the heavier side, because they are very sour crudes with higher viscosity levels. Collectively, the OPEC crude basket still correlates to and follows the WTI and Brent markets.

OPEC Crude Production

While OPEC doesn't officially release production targets, the market does follow informal production guidelines with interest. Generally, announcements (often

TABLE 12.1 OPEC Crude Oil Production Based on Secondary Sources (1,000 b/d)

Country	Crude Oil Production	Reference Crude
Algeria	1,265	Saharan Blend
Angola	1,785	Girassol
Ecuador	465	Oriente
Iran	3,688	Iran Heavy
Iraq	2,414	Basrah Light
Kuwait	2,315	Kuwait Export
Libya	1,556	Es Sider
Nigeria	2,242	Bonny Light
Qatar	810	Qatar Marine
Saudi Arabia	8,169	Arab Light
United Arab Emirates	2,311	Murban
Venezuela	2,284	Merey
Total	29,304	

Source: OPEC.
Note: As of October 2010.

released by third parties) of general production targets are helpful to the market. Market participants readily know OPEC's general intentions.

Historically, OPEC has had a checkered past when it comes to crude production compliance. For each member country, crude oil is the lifeblood of its respective economy. One can easily imagine as crude oil prices decline, so does the revenue of each country. How does a country reconcile cash shortfalls? More often than not, OPEC member countries produce more than their so-called production quotas. On the flip side, an OPEC country may take advantage of higher crude prices and try to produce more barrels of crude when favorable market conditions arise. Increased production typically happens as crude oil prices rise. Essentially, a member always has an incentive to produce beyond its quota. As a result, OPEC's compliance levels have varied to some degree. This situation has resulted in an erosion of OPEC's own compliance levels and some might argue its own credibility. Table 12.1 illustrates each OPEC country and its respective crude oil production levels.

OPEC's Role during the Financial Crisis 2008 to 2009

One can debate whether, during the financial crisis of 2008 to 2009, OPEC's role contributed to the recovery of crude oil prices. The cartel elected to decrease crude oil production in a series of four ensuing production cuts that began in the fourth quarter of 2008 and continued into early 2009. OPEC's reaction to the crude price collapse that began in 2008 was to announce crude oil production cuts totaling 4.2 mmbpd. OPEC implemented approximately 2.0 mmbpd in actual crude production cuts. During the course of 2009, OPEC maintained its production levels and did not elect to increase production. When crude prices rebounded in late 2009, OPEC still maintained its then-current production status of 24.845 mmbpd. What's different this time from prior price collapses?

One doesn't have to recall too far back when crude oil prices plummeted to nearly $10 per barrel in 1998. It begs the question as to why crude oil prices collapsed to nearly $10 per barrel in 1998, during the Asian crisis. Clearly, the economic crisis of 2008 to 2009 and the ensuing global economic recession was of a far greater scope and magnitude than the Asian crisis of 1998. Thirteen years ago, OPEC was not as cohesive an organization as it is today. In 2009, there was considerably greater OPEC unity among the membership. In addition, the crude oil inventory overhang was much greater in 1998 than in 2008 and 2009. In 1998, the crude oil inventory overhang was near 2.0 mmbpd. Overhang refers to a large build up of crude oil inventories. In 1998, implementing coordinated production cuts was a far greater challenge among the ranks of the OPEC membership. In 2009, I would also maintain that based on Table 12.1 that OPEC was clearly doing the heavy lifting for the industry by dramatically cutting its crude production in the first quarter of 2009. After the New York Mercantile Exchange (NYMEX) crude futures reached its record high, in July 2008 at $147 per barrel, non-OPEC producers slowly began to reduce crude production when commercial and industrial crude demand began to crater in the third and fourth quarter of 2008. Extreme crude prices were beginning to be felt by the industrial sector, airlines, transportation, and they reacted accordingly. Soon after, NYMEX futures prices began plummeting throughout the third and fourth quarter of 2008. By December 2008, crude prices were near $30 per barrel.

There is an interesting learning experience in market economics. The price elasticity of crude oil demand at $147 per barrel became readily measurable. As crude oil prices increased, the market reacted when cost structures began to soar in the commercial and industrial sectors. Airlines began to cut flights and trucking companies put fewer trucks on the road. Every commercial purchaser of gasoline and diesel cut back. Retail customers reduced consumption as well. According to the EIA, this is evidenced by a 900,000 bpd decrease in diesel fuel demanded in the 3Q and 4Q of 2008. OPEC took note. During the recession that ensued, OPEC appeared cognizant that any significant increase in crude prices could damage an already fragile global economic situation.

OPEC seemed committed to maintaining as high a crude price as was feasible under the difficult economic circumstances without triggering further global economic distress. While OPEC compliance is frequently questionable, 80 percent compliance did begin to place a bottom on crude oil prices and slowly lifted the market out of the $35-per-barrel range by the second and third quarter of 2009.

Interestingly enough, OPEC's Chapter 1 Article 2B states the purpose of its organization is to foremost meet the economic needs of member countries while also "ensuring the stabilization of prices in international oil markets with a view to eliminating harmful and unnecessary fluctuations." This is a very intriguing by-law considering the role OPEC played in this most recent economic crisis. Taking 2.0 million barrels per day off of the global market clearly helped oil industry producers by stabilizing crude prices considering that non-OPEC producers actually increased crude production in the fourth quarter 2008 and first quarter 2009.

However, by the end of 2009 when crude prices increased to $80 per barrel, the cartel publicly stated its satisfaction with crude prices at $70 per barrel. Given where prices were, $70 per barrel looked incredible. The industry could continue investing and be profitable at $70 per barrel. Throughout the second half of 2009, OPEC was rewarded with crude prices that were fairly resilient and remained in a $55 to $65 trading range. Despite $55 per barrel crude prices, independent oil companies still incurred 50 percent to 60 percent decreases in net earnings throughout most of 2009. Undoubtedly, 2008 and 2009 will be years to forget for the oil industry. As crude oil prices continue their upward ascent, OPEC has publicly announced its pleasure with the a crude oil price environment near $90 per barrel.

Saudi Arabia's Role in OPEC

Saudi Arabia is the largest crude oil producer in the world, currently producing approximately 8.0 million barrels per day. The Saudis have a unique role in the OPEC cartel. Because Saudi Arabia is the largest producer, its voice carries a great deal of political influence in OPEC. Some might argue that Saudi's voice can be heard beyond the confines of OPEC. Others might contend OPEC no longer matters in the marketplace.

As far as crude production is concerned, there are few, if any, producers that are capable of surpassing the Saudi's crude production. Quite simply, the Saudis remain the proverbial "big gorilla" in the crude oil marketplace. When OPEC commits to crude oil production cuts or increases, the Saudis will almost always take the brunt of production cuts. While such production cuts and increases are largely based on each country's pro rata share, the Saudi's are the ones to take the most significant hits when there are production decreases and first rewarded when there are production increases.

Quite simply, the Saudis can withstand the economic shock of production cuts. While production cuts adversely impact each member country, small OPEC members such as Ecuador are particularly vulnerable to production cuts. Despite an environment of weaker crude prices, Saudi Arabia is still able to maintain its investment programs.

Saudi Arabia has stated its commitment to maintaining "stability" in global oil prices by increasing its own crude production capacity. Most new crude oil demand stems from emerging market countries. Saudi Aramco (the state oil company of Saudi Arabia) has increased its crude oil production capacity to approximately 12.5 million barrels per day to meet increasing crude demand from emerging market economies, albeit only 8.0 mmbpd of production capacity is currently being utilized. Saudi Arabia has increased its production to make up for Libyan production disruption. According to OPEC, 10 member countries have a total of approximately $120 billion in upstream, refining, pipeline, terminal, and downstream investment projects.

OPEC versus Non-OPEC Reserves

OPEC member countries can lay claim to some of the most significant crude oil basins in the world. According to the *BP Statistical Review of World Energy June 2010*, Saudi Arabia is home to 263 billion barrels of crude oil reserves. See Figure 12.1. OPEC member countries have been diligently certifying their probable (2P) reserves and moving these reserves into the proven (1P) reserve category. According to the *BP Statistical Review of World Energy June 2010*, Venezuela has almost 172 billion barrels of 1P or proven reserves.

In the Western hemisphere, Venezuela is home to one of the largest crude basins, the Orinoco Belt. PDVSA has actively implemented a program aimed at certifying its crude reserves. This has led to a great deal of interest in its reserves

FIGURE 12.1   Figure Reserves Chart

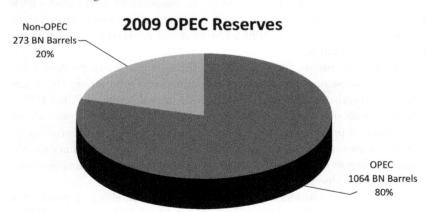

Source: OPEC.

among the global oil community. However, the Chavez administration began a campaign of nationalizing numerous industries including the oil and gas industry. This has had a dampening effect on investment in Venezuela.

According to OPEC, member countries possess 79.6 percent of the world's reserves, or 1,064 BOE as of 2010. This is a staggering number. It leaves independent oil companies in the difficult situation of working with countries with challenging geopolitical situations or less-than-desirable contractual arrangements.

For non-OPEC countries, this situation should be a wake-up call. There is increasing "resource nationalization" in the industry. For independent producers, this is another wrinkle to the global natural resource dilemma. Countries such as Norway, Russia, Mexico, and Brazil have considerable crude oil reserves. However, most of these countries have implemented varying forms of concession or production-sharing agreements with very favorable terms for the state-owned oil company. There are limitations as to whether an independent oil company can book reserves in an open and competitive concession production-sharing contract format. Brazil did permit concession contracts until new Brazilian energy laws were proposed in late 2009 on the heels of the pre-salt discoveries in the South Atlantic.

Geopolitics of Crude

Among the 12 OPEC members, some countries have proven themselves to be better places to operate than other countries. In 2007, a wave of nationalization in Ecuador and Venezuela resulted in independent oil companies departing from both countries. Interestingly, state oil companies are continuing to show an interest in Venezuela. We believe that reserves are the end game. If a country has certified reserves, it is in the game.

However, the whole notion of contract sanctity comes in to play here. Both Ecuador and Venezuela have regulatory regimes that have resulted in higher royalties being paid to the state. In January 2007, Venezuela implemented its Empresas Mixtas policy which states that PDVSA must have at least a 60 percent participation in any project. Ecuador implemented royalties north of 90 percent to be paid to the state. The result of this is a diminished level of investment in both countries.

Nationalization of Assets

In recent years, there are increasing acts of blatant confiscation and nationalization of energy-sector assets. Needless to say, the energy sector has taken note and independents are staying out of markets such as Ecuador, Bolivia, and Venezuela.

While Ecuador and Bolivia are smaller markets, Venezuela previously had considerable appeal. Over time, confiscation of assets and the takeover of whole industries will have a chilling effect on investment and growth. Venezuela is already witnessing a decline in investment as the energy sector grapples with electricity shortages and an aging infrastructure.

Concluding Thoughts

OPEC has evolved and become increasingly media savvy. More importantly, OPEC appears to be keenly aware of the effects of its policy on the global market. As crude prices continue their ascent, there is growing contentment with prevailing market conditions among the OPEC membership. No surprise. But if the crude markets continue to climb on the heels of inflation-increasing government policies, we may yet see OPEC move in a different direction. To date, crude oil inventories have been well above the five-year averages. Given ample crude supplies, OPEC is not likely to make any production changes in the near term despite triple digit crude oil prices. For the moment, Saudi Arabia has become the swing producer as it steps in to fill production gaps as Middle East contagion spreads. So far, Saudi Arabia has been able to fulfill Libya's 1.5 mmbpd production quota.

CHAPTER 13

Bidding and Production Rights

Oil-producing nations each have their own set of laws and regulatory frameworks by which other nations and private companies may participate. Some countries, such as Brazil and Norway, are very progressive in their energy models. Others, such as Venezuela, are considerably more restrictive. Below, we will review some differences and similarities across business models and energy frameworks.

Brazil

The South Atlantic has become one of the hottest locales in the global oil industry with the 2007 discovery of the Lula (formerly known as Tupi) field off the coast of Brazil. The Lula field was discovered by a consortium consisting of Petrobras, Portugal's Galp Energia S.A., and the U.K.'s BG Group Plc. Petrobras is operator and has considerable technological expertise in deepwater drilling.

Currently, the Lula field (block BMS-11) is estimated to have approximately five to six billion BOE in the Santos basin. Other neighboring blocks in both the Santos and Campos basins have since been determined to have significant reserve potential. For Petrobras, this may translate to an increase in proven reserves from what is approximately 14 billion BOE (according to company data per SPE criteria) to reserves as high as 20 to 25 billion BOE, including new fields in both the Campos and Santos basins—over the next decade. As of October 2009, Brazil has approximately 77 concession agreements in effect.

As a result of the major oil discovery, Brazil's government has decided to change its energy laws and discontinue the previous concession model for any field deemed to be *in a key strategic area*. What is considered strategic? It is virtually any offshore field. Since the Lula discovery, Brazil's Petrobras has made numerous other hydrocarbon discoveries in nearby fields with similar geologic

119

characteristics and structures. Based on the company's public assessment of the discovery and the disclosure that BMS-11 was formed during the prehistoric continental shift between South America and the African continent, it is not unreasonable for scientists to predict that the possibility exists for hydrocarbons to exist in other nearby offshore fields. Numerous discoveries have since been made in neighboring fields. Petrobras's and other global operators' track record certainly supports the potential geological hypothesis.

Whether it is good genes or good geology, the fact remains that neither can easily be replicated. We are born with our own genetic makeup. Similarly, hydrocarbons have formed thousands of meters below the pre-salt layers, off the coast of Brazil, as organic matter decomposed over millions of years in the ocean floor. Simply put, you either have good geology or you don't. If a country is not fortunate enough to have good geology, its global oil producers will continue to have to work with host countries and work through a variety of concession agreements, production contracts, and the like to develop and exploit crude-bearing fields.

So while the global oil industry tries to determine whether the new Brazilian energy framework will result in more or less opportunity for producers, a few items still remain worthy of consideration. Petrobras takes on a more significant role in the Brazilian petroleum sector. More importantly, Brazil can lay claim to the largest crude oil discovery in the Americas since the Cantarell discovery in the Gulf of Mexico in the 1970s by PEMEX.

Geology Matters

The bottom line is there is no substitute for the extraordinary geology that exists thousands of meters below the ocean floor in the South Atlantic. After 30 years, the Cantarell basin is now in its twilight. The Lula field has produced first oil and can lay claim to approximately 6 billion boe. The Brazilian Agência Nacional do Petróleo (ANP) places impressive potential reserve estimates on the neighboring fields of Libra, Iara, Guara, Franco, and others. In the aggregate, the ANP has preliminarily estimated hydrocarbons in excess of 25 to 30 billion barrels. Consequently, Brazil has become a very appealing investment prospect.

Government Participation

There is no doubt that the Brazilian government intends to increase its ownership of Petrobras amidst the once-in-a-generation pre-salt discovery in the South Atlantic. As the new energy framework is outlined—Petrobras will be the operator in all offshore fields—with a minimum 30 percent participation, determined to be in each *key strategic area*. Given the fact that the size of the pre-salt blocks is nearly that of the Gulf of Mexico, Petrobras will undoubtedly need partners and resources to develop these fields. Petrobras has expertise in deepwater drilling and knowledge of these fields like no other global producer. At this juncture, Petrobras is a desirable business partner despite the fact that the Brazilian government has increased its ownership to approximately 60 percent. Independent oil companies and investors interested in Brazil will have to get comfortable with that notion and everything it represents.

The Role of Government

Brazil represents a unique place in the global oil and gas industry. Democracy and capital markets are alive and well in Brazil. That is not the case in all geographies where hydrocarbons are present. The Middle East, Nigeria, and Russia all beckon with opportunity, but the institutions or lack thereof make these geographies an uncertain bet at best. The institutions of democracy, the rule of law, and a vibrant capital market system enable Brazil to attract not only investment in a growing energy sector, but home building, petrochemicals, airlines, pulp, media, and other industries have grown considerably over the past five years.

The Brazilian economy has been very resilient compared to other major economies of Europe and the United States. While the financial crisis has resulted in the first Brazilian recession since 2003, the Brazilian central bank took swift action to ensure liquidity and stabilize financial markets. This crisis did not have the impact on the Brazilian economy compared to some of its neighbors. On the contrary, the Brazilian economy has fared quite well with expected GDP growth of approximately 7 percent expected for 2011. The end game is that Brazil represents a unique opportunity in a very appealing geography, infrastructure, and political environment for the global oil industry.

Mexico

Recent discoveries in the Gulf of Mexico prove an interesting situation. The recent Tiber discovery by BP illustrates that various geologic shelf structures in the Gulf once thought to be dormant contain considerable development potential. Another discovery by McMoRan in the shallow waters of the Gulf of Mexico illustrates the opportunities right in the backyard of both the United States and Mexico. This is a wake-up for call for both the United States and Mexico seeking exploration opportunities.

On the Mexican side of the Gulf of Mexico, the Cantarell crude oil basin is in its natural decline. In 1999, Mexico was producing 3.3 mmbpd of crude oil. Today, state-owned Mexican oil company Petróleos Mexicanos (PEMEX) is producing approximately 2.9 mmbpd (according to the *BP Statistical Review of World Energy June 2010*) of crude in Cantarell. Approximately 80 percent of Mexican crude oil is exported to the United States. This supply is declining

TABLE 13.1 Crude Oil Production by Country (millions of barrels per day)

Country	1999	2009	Percentage +/−
United States	7.731	7.196	(6.92%)
Mexico	3.343	2.979	(10.89%)
Norway	3.139	2.342	(25.39%)
United Kingdom	2.909	1.448	(50.22%)
Brazil	1.133	2.029	79.08%
Venezuela	3.126	2.437	(22.04%)

Source: BP Statistical Review of World Energy June 2010.

perhaps more quickly than most energy analysts anticipated. The challenges of replenishing supply and mitigating the current decline are considerable for PEMEX and the Mexican government.

In October 2008, the Mexican government passed its Energy Reform bill aimed at giving PEMEX more exploration autonomy. While the legislation was needed, it didn't quite go far enough. The energy reform bill provided for greater transparencies, corporate governance initiatives, and greater budgetary control. However, the legislation maintained the existing service-provider contracts. The global oil and gas industry was hoping for a more progressive structure such as a concession model enabling global producers to come to Mexico, work with PEMEX, and bid on concession projects.

Under a concession model, producers are generally able to book hydrocarbon reserves as their own. Under service provider contracts, global producers and service-sector companies are invited to work alongside PEMEX but unable to book reserves. This work is generally project-related work and nothing more. This policy has resulted in muted interest in Mexican oil fields. The policy has since been improved to attract greater interest in Mexico. Table 13.2 depicts the gradual decline in crude oil production by major producers. Brazil is the only growth story amongst this group.

As previously mentioned, the whole notion of resource nationalization is prevalent in Mexico. The current administration has to convince the Mexican public that bringing in global producers is really in its interest. There is no doubt that both the current administration and PEMEX executive management know and recognize this all too well. This is a complex situation with its history grounded almost 70 years ago when oil was first discovered in Mexico. Full participation in the Mexican petroleum industry requires constitutional change—which is not likely to take place anytime soon. The Mexican public is largely influenced by the opposing political party, ensuring the electorate fears global participation in their crude oil industry.

The result is no one wins. Mexican crude oil production is declining as illustrated above, and PEMEX is fairly constrained as to what it can do to improve the situation. A significant change in energy policy would require constitutional change, which is highly unlikely. While another energy reform may be in the works, it is only speculation at this writing. What happens next may also be influenced by Mexican elections and the opposition's determination to adversely influence the electorate. For any producer, growing the reserve and production base is a long, expensive, and arduous process requiring a multitude of global partners. Over the next several years, the Mexican government will be challenged to curtail the decline in crude oil production and renew growth.

Norway

Oil production in Norway has been very active for more than 40 years. In recent years, North Sea oil production has reached its maturity and begun its natural decline. According to the *BP Statistical Review of World Energy June 2010*, Norwegian crude oil production in 1999 was 3.139 million barrels per day. In 2009, Norway produced 2.3 million barrels per day. In 2010, Norway's state-owned Statoil Hydro produced approximately 1.7 mmbpd of Norway's total 2.1 mmbpd crude oil production (according to company data at www.statoil.com). Over the last two decades, Norway's crude oil production and proven crude oil reserves have steadily declined as its fields have matured. Table 13.2 illustrates the decline in crude oil reserves among many major producers. Venezuela and Brazil are the exception with considerable proven reserve growth.

Therein lays the challenge for Norway to structure and attract continued investment while production and reserves are well into their natural decline. Unlike Mexico, outside third-party investment is welcome to participate in the bid rounds. In Norway's 2010 Awards in Predefined Areas (APA), 41 companies from all over the globe participated. Even though many areas on the Norwegian

TABLE 13.2 Proven Crude Oil Reserves by Country (billions of barrels)

Country	1989	1999	2009
United States	34.3	29.7	28.4
Mexico	52.0	21.5	11.9
Norway	8.4	10.9	7.1
United Kingdom	3.8	5.0	3.1
Brazil	2.8	8.2	12.9
Venezuela	59.0	76.8	172.3

Source: BP Statistical Review of World Energy June 2010.

shelf are considered mature, Norway is able to structure its bid rounds to continue to attract investment from both large and small global oil companies.

With current crude oil prices relatively high, smaller oil companies may find mature basins attractive if they have the enhanced recovery technology. In addition, mature areas still have access to existing infrastructure and have the potential to develop more quickly than new areas on the Norwegian shelf. The time necessary to develop a field is always a consideration for the smaller oil company, where the economics play a more significant role. Smaller oil companies are much more vulnerable to a downturn in commodity prices.

In the 2010 bid round, 41 companies were vying for 22,600 square kilometers across 63 blocks. Because there are mature areas on the Norwegian shelf, the APA is managing the bid rounds to ensure that fields are always being turned over. The key is managing the natural decline of mature fields. Norway's policy has been effective in dealing with mature fields and declining production.

The Norwegian model provides for state participation per the Norwegian Petroleum Activities Act Section 1-1 which states "the Norwegian State has the proprietary right to subsea petroleum deposits and the exclusive right to resource management." The Act further states that "the State reserves a specified share of a license granted pursuant to this Act and in the joint venture established by a joint operating agreement in accordance with the license." Today, Norway owns approximately 67 percent of Statoil with global investors owning the remainder.

The Act (according to Section 3-6) further states that the Norwegian King "may decide that the Norwegian State shall participate in petroleum activities according to this Act." While Norway owns and participates in the oil and gas exploration, it has successfully structured its energy policy to attract considerable outside investment while faced with the challenge of turning around its mature production fields.

The United Kingdom

The United Kingdom faces a challenge similar to that of Norway. Over a decade ago, UK crude oil production peaked at more than 3.0 million barrels per day. Many areas of the UK continental shelf are similarly in their natural decline. Such mature fields are still of interest to many smaller firms and those with enhanced recovery technology. Over the last 40 years, UK bid rounds have attracted interest from independent oil companies (IOCs) all over the globe and continue to do so today.

The UK Department of Energy and Climate Change (DECC) is the authority that regulates all offshore drilling activity and is keenly aware of the importance that energy plays in the greater UK economy and its national security. In addition, because the United Kingdom is a net importer of both crude oil and natural gas, efforts to revitalize mature areas and develop newer areas of the UK Continental Shelf are of strategic importance.

UK authorities, in addition to other nations, have watched and learned from the 2010 BP Gulf of Mexico oil spill. The UK DECC estimates approximately 40 billion BOE have been produced over the last several decades. However, DECC estimates there are approximately 20 billion BOE remaining to be produced. DECC further states that deepwater oil and natural gas potential is estimated at 3.0 to 3.5 billion BOE or 15 to 17.5 percent of total resources.

The United Kingdom has not curtailed deepwater exploration and continues to issue deepwater licenses. UK authorities have reiterated their commitment to safety and regulatory precautions currently in place with which operators must comply. Nevertheless, DECC and other authorities continue to study the Gulf of Mexico investigation. UK authorities have established a joint industry and governmental organization, the Oil Spill Prevention and Response Advisory Group (OSPRAG), which has instituted the following five interim compliance measures for operators.

1. Action to double the number of annual environmental inspections by DECC to drilling rigs including the appointment of three additional inspectors.
2. Launch of a new joint advisory group OSPRAG to review the United Kingdom's ability to prevent and respond to oil spills.
3. Award a contract to Wood Group Kenny for the design of a new oil spill mitigation technology for the UK Continental Shelf.
4. Study estimates of the cost of an oil-spill cleanup in the United Kingdom.
5. Bring forward the planned testing of the National Contingency Plan, and its interaction with other major incident plans, including the oil pollution emergency plans submitted by operators of offshore installations, with a major oil pollution exercise in 2011.

To date, the United Kingdom's deepest well is in 1,900 meters of water whereas the BP Macondo well was drilled in 1,520 meters of water. The United Kingdom is not implementing a moratorium on deepwater drilling, citing numerous safety precautions and a robust regulatory regime designed to work with operators on ensuring safety and environmental protections.

The United Kingdom's bid rounds are designed to ensure continued interest and participation by global energy companies despite many mature fields. According to DECC (www.decc.gov.uk), future areas of oil and gas exploration may include UK Continental Shelf to the west of Scotland, where water depth is in excess of 3,000 meters.

Venezuela

Petróleos de Venezuela S.A. (PDVSA) is an institution that has considerable potential. It can lay claim to some of the world's largest crude oil reserves outside of the Middle East and Canada. According to the *BP Statistical Review of World*

Energy June 2010, Venezuela's proven reserves are 172 billion BOE. According to 2009 company data, there are 2P reserves of approximately 95 billion BOE.

In 2007, PDVSA's energy policy was revised and steps taken to nationalize the energy sector. Over the last several years, additional steps have been taken to further nationalize the oilfield service sector and other industries. The core of the energy policy establishes PDVSA as having a 60 percent interest in any project. The energy policy known as Empresas Mixtas establishes further governmental control on the oil and gas sector. Royalties and taxes have been increased as payments to the state are now considerable when compared to other nations.

When the new energy policy was adopted in 2007, many independent oil companies chose to leave Venezuela as projects in the Orinoco Belt were nationalized to a great deal of media coverage. ExxonMobil and ConocoPhillips were among those companies choosing to leave Venezuela. However, many other companies chose to stay.

Despite the fact that it has now been several years since the nationalization took place, Venezuela is still able to attract outside interest in its bid rounds. Most participating companies are state-owned institutions. Interestingly Chevron and Repsol won a recent bid round.

Venezuela is challenged to attract and maintain interest in Venezuela's heavy crude oil basin known as the Orinoco Belt or the Faja as it is known in Venezuela. The heavier, sour crude needs upgrading prior to refining, but Venezuela is home to massive amounts of reserves. The majors recognize these dynamics, but many companies will be hesitant to participate because of known risks. However, national oil companies (NOCs) don't appear to be bothered by the issues associated with greater state control.

Concluding Thoughts

When comparing bid rounds and energy policy across the globe, Venezuela is at the extreme when compared to Norway or Brazil. Norway and Brazil are at the forefront of attracting outside investment. Other smaller countries such as Colombia and Peru have some of the most progressive energy frameworks in the Americas. Colombia and Peru each have more than 60 concessions in operation. The smaller countries and larger countries discussed here are excellent examples of the benefits of greater market participation. Undoubtedly, government policy matters. Energy frameworks can either attract investment opportunities or discourage them. We reviewed some excellent examples of progressive energy frameworks and reviewed instances of more challenged regimes.

CHAPTER 14

Analyzing State-Owned Oil Companies

State-owned oil companies are not all alike. While they have many similarities, there are some differences that are noteworthy. State-owned oil companies are as varied as the oil they produce. While all are owned by their governments, they differ by the percentage of government ownership.

In some cases, both governments and investors own these complex corporations. We refer to these entities as mixed-capital companies. These institutions are held to the standards of a private company, but have the complexity of two sets of owners, its government and global investors. This chapter provides a roadmap to understanding these structures and how they differ from the state-owned oil company which is entirely owned by its government.

Hydrocarbons, a Source of Revenue

Among state-owned oil companies, a common denominator is the reliance on crude and natural gas production as a key source of revenue to its domestic economy. When crude oil or natural gas prices significantly decline, these economies are weakened. In a declining crude and natural gas price environment, national oil companies (NOCs) tend to react differently. Smaller countries have less flexibility and financial resources to withstand such economic shocks. Countries such as Ecuador and Venezuela rely on crude oil production as their economic lifeline.

As another example, Mexico has tried to increase its revenue base by increasing taxes among the corporate sector. Venezuela has been reticent to increase taxes among the electorate. Therein lays the challenge of balancing economic policy with ever-shifting commodity prices. Economies such as Saudi Arabia can easily withstand periodic downturns in crude oil prices. Smaller economies,

TABLE 14.1   2009 Crude Oil Production and Exports as a Percent of GDP

Country	2009 Crude Oil Production (mmbpd)	Export % of GDP 2009
Venezuela	2.43	18%
Saudi Arabia	9.71	53%
Mexico	2.97	28%
Ecuador	0.49	37%

Source: World Bank and BP Statistical Review of World Energy June 2010.

such as Ecuador, endure much difficulty in long downturns in crude oil prices. Table 14.1 illustrates hydrocarbon production for four oil-producing countries and total exports as a percent of gross domestic product (GDP). The majority of exports of the Latin American countries are generally crude oil, refined products, and to a lesser degree, agriculture. Certainly, the majority of Saudi Arabia's exports are crude oil.

Regulatory Frameworks

Sovereigns that are interested in attracting outside investment have opened up their regulatory frameworks and encouraged exploration and development work by outside private corporations.

Smaller countries such as Colombia and Peru have aggressively liberalized their energy framework to outside investment. This practice has proven economically beneficial to both countries. As a result, Colombia and Peru have approximately 75 concessions operating in each country, and both countries have permitted outside investors in oil and gas to repatriate funds and assets back to their home countries. The Colombian and Peruvian governments have actively courted the energy sector in North America and Europe. Later in this chapter we will review various regulatory frameworks and stipulations surrounding bid rounds.

As a result, there is a very robust energy sector with increasing crude oil production. Colombia has arrested its production decline and completely reversed the production picture to one of growth. Peru has a more liberalized energy framework than Colombia. In other words, if you like doing business in Colombia, you may like Peru even better. These relatively small countries have managed to return domestic crude and natural gas production to one of growth and increased business investment in the energy sector. The Canadian Free trade agreement has resulted in a plethora of Canadian companies that today have a very significant presence in Colombia.

Concessions and Bid Rounds

Concessionary frameworks vary to a wide degree by country. Countries such as Saudi Arabia prohibit independent oil companies (IOCs) from drilling and booking reserves for their own account. This doesn't mean that NOCs do not enter into partnerships with IOCs. NOCs certainly have an interest in various joint ventures, such as building refineries and pipelines to name a few. Where things get complex is the practice of booking reserves. Many sovereigns simply do not permit IOCs to drill and book hydrocarbon reserves.

The issue of booking reserves is more complex among mixed-capital companies. To a certain extent, mixed-capital companies permit oil and gas companies to book reserves. However, the oil and gas frameworks vary to a large degree even among mixed-capital companies. Every country differs to some degree and some are more inviting of the international oil and gas community.

The home government still has significant influence and sets the framework regarding bid rounds. The oil and gas (or energy) regulator will develop the rules, determine blocks for bidding, set parameters, and determine winners. Mixed-capital companies hold a very large allure because they generally are business friendly. As one would expect, many of the host governments provide for preferential treatment of their own state-owned oil companies. Examples of this are Brazil and Norway. Other countries with mixed-capital state-owned oil companies, such as Colombia, have completely liberalized their energy frameworks, permitting outside energy companies to participate and book reserves.

Taxes and Royalties

Every country has its own regulatory framework which producers are required to follow. Similarly, tax structures vary by country. Typically, state-owned oil companies pay hefty tax bills to the sovereign. Tax rates can range from 50 percent to almost 75 percent of annual earnings being paid to the sovereign. When crude oil prices decline, tax revenues similarly decline. Historically, PEMEX (Mexico's NOC) is an NOC that has had one of the highest corporate tax rates of any oil company. PEMEX has had years where its tax bill was approximately 75 percent of pre-tax earnings. This number has varied by the various tax regimes applied. The effect is noteworthy in that significant funds are paid to the state instead of being re-invested in the company or its infrastructure.

Pensions and Legacy Support

Many NOCs have well-established pension funds and legacy support systems for employees of state-owned production companies. The challenge becomes clear that the state supports a legion of former employees and transfers these mounting costs from state-owned oil producing companies. Many of these pension systems are underfunded and warrant careful scrutiny by investors. Pension benefit obligations are exactly that, an obligation or a liability of the NOC, and just another form of debt.

NOCs often have legacy payment structures that continue long after a given employee has left or retired from the production company. Many NOCs have the General Motors' problem of generations of employees and their families still receiving a plethora of benefits from the state-owned oil companies. For fixed income investors, this is an important part of the leverage analysis of NOCs.

Transparency

NOCs are often reticent to publish information in a comparable manner to that of IOCs. For investors who wish to conduct their own research, one simply may not find an abundance of information on closely held NOCs outside of what is already in the public domain. Unless the NOC has publicly issued bonds, investors may not be able to readily conduct research on a given state-owned oil company.

Some state-owned oil companies, such as PEMEX, will publish information for their global bond investors. PEMEX taps the capital markets on a regular basis and provides an outstanding level of information for global investors both in terms of quantity and quality. Annually, PEMEX publishes an entire book dedicated to the status of its hydrocarbon reserves and certification process. Its web site is first-rate and their investor relations team does a great job of reaching out to the investment community. PEMEX is an example of an exceptional level of transparency to investors and interested constituents around the globe.

Social Programs

NOCs are often required to contribute to the economic well being of the population. Many state-owned oil companies contribute a substantial portion of their annual earnings to fund social programs. PDVSA contributes approximately 40 percent (or more) of its pre-tax net earnings to Venezuela's domestic economy in taxes and has consistently done so for many years.

The downside to that situation is the lack of investment a company such as PDVSA can make in its own infrastructure. One can argue the economic disadvantages of forcing a state-owned oil and gas production company to fund health care and education programs instead of investing in refining capacity or reducing debt. This is often part of the business model of NOCs.

Capital Markets

Many NOCs have public bond issuances which require a credit rating from one of the rating agencies. This process has required that NOCs publish a certain level of financial disclosures in order to comply with SEC regulations for bond issuances in the United States. Consequently, investors have access to information from NOCs such as PEMEX, which regularly accesses the capital markets. Most Middle Eastern NOCs do not have such bond issuances. As a result, there is considerably less information on them available to outside investors.

The capital markets have proven to be a very valuable vehicle for some state-owned oil companies to shore up balance sheets by increasing liquidity, reducing leverage, or investing in infrastructure projects.

Mexico's PEMEX

Mexico has a long history in the hydrocarbon industry with production beginning in the 1930s. Oil was first discovered in 1939 in the once prolific Cantarell Basin on the Mexican side of the Gulf of Mexico. Crude oil production reached approximately 3.3 mmpd at its peak. Today, crude oil production is in the 2.4 to 2.8 mmpd range (according to company data). The challenge for PEMEX is its key basin is well into its natural decline and is now considered very mature. Enhanced recovery methods utilizing nitrogen are commonplace in the Cantarell basin in order to increase crude flow from existing wells.

What are equally important are the Mexican government's ownership and energy framework policies. Over the decades, the Mexican government has seldom opened its doors to outside investment. The integrated majors would be interested in the Mexican market if they could go there with the expectation of being able to drill and book reserves for their own accounts. As it stands, the Mexican Congress would require a constitutional change to permit outside investment in Mexican shores. As of the printing of this book, a constitutional change has not taken place and is not likely. However, minor policy changes have been implemented.

Over the years, the Mexican Congress has passed various tax and energy framework policies. Most of these regimes have sought to provide PEMEX with greater autonomy and reduce its corporate tax rate. The 2008 Energy Regime provided PEMEX with greater flexibility in budgeting, corporate planning, pro-curement, and corporate governance. While all very important, the congress has marginally accomplished what PEMEX needed the most—the ability to attract outside investment. This is particularly concerning given that its marquis field Cantarell is in its natural decline and reserves are not growing.

Ownership Structure

In most cases, the sovereign owns 100 percent of state-owned production companies such as Saudi Aramco or the Kuwait National Oil company. The sovereign owns the mineral rights and determines participation in the energy sector. Below we will review another form of ownership structure among NOCs such as hybrid or mixed-capital ownership structures. In a mixed-capital or hybrid structure, ownership is held by both the sovereign and outside investors.

Hybrid-Capital Companies

The other form of NOCs that warrants attention is those with hybrid-capital structures. This business model is the NOC that is jointly owned by the sovereign and outside investors.

Some of the best examples are Petrobras and Colombia's Ecopetrol. Both companies have a mixture of investors that own the public portions of each company. The sovereign government generally owns the majority of its NOC's publicly issued common stock. Refer to Table 14.2 for financial metrics of three unique mixed-capital companies. Petrobras has common stock that trades on the Brazilian Bovespa and American Depository Receipts (ADRs) that trade on the New York Stock Exchange (NYSE). Petrobras's investors are primarily large global institutional investors.

TABLE 14.2 Mixed-Capital Companies As of LTM September 2010

Company	Market Cap (USMM)	Est. State* Ownership	Country	Revenue (USDMM)	EBITDA (USMM)	Ave. Daily Oil Equiv. Prod. (mmboe)
Statoil	$74,773	67.2%	Norway	$85,853	$28,993	1.72
Petrobras	$225,134	21.9%	Brazil	$123,929	$38,231	2.58
Ecopetrol	$83,314	89.9%	Colombia	$19,737	$7,233	0.62

Source: Copyright © Capital IQ, Inc, a Standard & Poor's business. Standard & Poor's including its subsidiary corporations is a division of The McGraw Hill Companies, Inc. Reproduction of this Chart in any form is prohibited without Capital IQ, Inc.'s prior written permission.
Note: All data as of most recent financial statements reported.
*As defined by Capital IQ consisting of common stock equivalent held.

Accountability

Hybrid-capital structure companies are accountable not only to their home governments, but a legion of global investors. Their responsibilities for financial disclosure are considerable and mirror that of their privately held counterparts. The hybrid form capital structure companies have sophisticated investor relations teams who are the vital link to the investment community. Their behavior with investors is similar to that of any other publicly held corporation and these companies are held to the same regulatory standards as privately held companies.

Mixed-capital companies have instituted and internalized the demands of being a public company and institutionalized the rigors associated with financial reporting, regulatory compliance, and demands of exchanges and investors. Petrobras is one of the best examples of a mixed-capital company that has been embraced by the international capital markets over and over again. Petrobras has adopted Sarbanes-Oxley 404 and 414 regulations because it issues ADRs in the United States and has to abide by Securities and Exchange Commission (SEC) regulations. As such, Petrobras is at the forefront of what can be achieved by a mixed-capital company and has truly raised the bar.

Transparency

Because mixed-capital companies frequently tap the capital markets, there is a continual level of information and disclosure available to global investors. As such, these companies have to be as transparent as that of their publicly held counterparts. In many cases, there is still a considerable level of government influence. It would not be characteristic to completely eliminate government intervention, but it is more manageable.

Access to Capital

The most significant benefit to a hybrid- or mixed-capital structure is access to global capital markets. For most of these companies, the benefit is significant. For instance, Petrobras has been able to grow its capital expenditures and crude oil production-based initiatives by virtue of its access to global capital markets. There is always healthy investor demand and interest in the mixed-capital companies for all of the obvious reasons.

Both the equity and fixed income markets have proven to be advantageous to companies with mixed-capital structures. Equity is every company's friend. Shoring up the balance sheet with new equity is often a very strategic solution to funding future growth. By virtue of their ownership structures, most NOCs can only access the fixed income market. While this is beneficial in refinancing existing higher-priced bonds, the equity markets offer an additional layer of financial flexibility.

Not the Primary Source of Domestic GDP

In general, mixed-capital companies are not the primary source of revenue for their respective domestic economies. In the case of Brazil, the domestic economy consists of many large industrial sectors such as petrochemical, home building, agribusiness, airline, and ethanol production. Brazil's economy is not completely dependent upon the oil and gas sector. Petrobras pays corporate taxes, but it is not the sole source of domestic revenue. There is no question that a strong oil and gas sector has contributed to larger domestic expansion.

Countries such as Colombia and Peru also have increasingly active capital and banking markets. This has been an engine of growth for two small countries with robust and growing domestic capital markets

U.S. SarBox laws

Companies with hybrid-capital structures conform to U.S. Sarbanes-Oxley (SarBox) laws if they issue securities in U.S. markets. This is a considerable comfort for investors seeking security of additional disclosures by foreign issuers. SarBox regulations require that any foreign-owned oil, gas, or energy company has to comply with various financial and accounting related disclosures including the management certifications (both CFO and CEO signatures) on financial statements. In addition, these companies have to comply with the internal audit and compliance requirements. As such, hybrid-capital companies have had to institutionalize these demands. This is another layer of disclosure compliance through which investors can find comfort.

Corporate Tax Structure

Corporate tax structures are not excessive for hybrid-capital companies compared to many NOCs. Hybrid-capital companies tend to have corporate tax structures that are comparable to other publicly held companies in the 30 percent to 40 percent range. Mixed-capital companies are not supporting the weight of their domestic economies. These companies are not funding large-scale social spending and public programs. As such, these companies are able to invest and earn healthy levels of profitability.

Many NOCs are further taxed with excessive royalties that are paid to home governments. In weak crude oil-price environments, the combination of excessive corporate taxes and royalties are enough to burden many NOCs. The result has been that mixed-capital companies have a good track record of investment and capital expenditure planning. In other words, they are aggressively investing in the business and not constrained by sovereign burdens. Consequently, many of these companies can become very competitive with IOCs relative to their more burdened NOC counterparts.

Role of the Chairman and CEO

Many NOCs have one individual who fills the role of both Chairman and CEO. Often times, that role would also be that of the Energy Minister. Mixed-capital companies have taken steps to institute a separation of the two offices by ensuring those positions are held by different individuals. There is no surprise that global investors prefer this separation of powers.

Norway

For mixed-capital companies, Norway's Statoil has become the business model of the energy industry. Statoil (OB:STL) has set the benchmark by which many other oil and gas companies seek to be measured. Statoil has successfully bridged the challenges associated with both private and public ownership. In June 2001, Statoil was one of the first state-owned global oil companies to execute an initial public offering and became a public company. Statoil has since set the benchmark and the standard for a new model of corporate governance. Today, Statoil's marquis blocks are in their maturity. While still prolific, crude oil production growth is increasingly a challenge.

Statoil Hydro is an example of a mixed-capital structure company, whereby the Norwegian government owns 67.2 percent of the equity and global investors hold the remainder. More importantly, Statoil Hydro developed the model by which Brazil's Petrobras and Colombia's Ecopetrol subsequently modeled aspects of their corporate governance and domestic energy policy. The success of the hybrid-capital structure is due in part to the road paved by Statoil Hydro in bringing together private investors and government. Today, this business model is still successful.

Brazil

The growth of the Brazilian oil and gas sector can make a very interesting business school case study of what a state-owned oil company can achieve if it has access to capital markets. Many years ago, Brazil liberalized its energy sector by allowing outside investment in Brazilian assets. Under the previous energy regulatory framework, Brazil would hold its bid rounds and outside companies would bid for a position as part of a consortium to develop a given field.

In 2010, the Brazilian government changed its energy framework to a model similar to that of Norway. The Brazilian state-owned oil company Petrobras (BOVESPA:PBR4), would now have a 30 percent participation in areas defined as key strategic areas by the Brazilian regulator, ANP. The key strategic areas are deepwater fields offshore of Rio de Janeiro and Sao Paulo. The result is still considerable industry interest in the South Atlantic basins of Santos where new fields hold significant amounts of hydrocarbons. According to Petrobras, the newly named Lula and Iracema fields hold approximately 6.5 and 1.8 billion BOE, respectively.

Colombia

Colombia is a phenomenal study in what can be achieved by any country, not just a smaller country. Colombia's state-owned oil and gas company Ecopetrol (BVC:ECOPETROL) is the classic example of a smaller company very successfully doing large-company things. No one can dispute the success that Ecopetrol had when it decided to become a publicly-traded corporation. Since then, additional access to capital has been made available to Ecopetrol by being able to access funds in the global capital markets. Today, Ecopetrol is owned by both the Colombian government and global investors and a successful example of the benefits of being a hybrid-capital structure company.

Not only has an initial public issuance been very beneficial for Ecopetrol, but certainly the liberalization of Colombia's energy framework resulted in approximately 75 concessions now operating in Colombia. Colombia is considered small-company friendly and has become a haven for small- and-mid-cap oil and gas companies seeking to explore and develop fields in Colombia. In a given country, the energy framework makes the difference between energy growth and stagnation. In this case, under the tutelage of Colombia's President Uribe, Colombia got it right.

Concluding Thoughts

We reviewed three fascinating companies, Statoil, Petrobras, and Ecopetrol that are held to public-company standards yet are still majority owned by their governments. Within the context of their ownership structure, they are able to grow, raise funds, and have a level of transparency not often found with state-owned companies. We believe all three companies offer appealing opportunities to investors.

CHAPTER 15

Crude Oil Pricing and Industry Investment

The years 2008 and 2009 were unlike any other in the crude oil markets. In July 2008, crude oil prices closed at a historic high of $147 per barrel on the NYMEX. By December 2008, crude oil prices plummeted to near $30 per barrel. Both extremes in crude oil pricing took place within a six-month time frame. This chapter reviews some of the events leading up to the historic market and economic events of the financial crisis and its impact on the crude oil markets. However, record crude oil prices were not without consequences and its effects were amplified by the coincident crises in the global credit markets by late 2008.

This chapter puts some of these historic market events in perspective. We also look forward and assess whether the market has the ability to return to triple-digit crude prices. Finally, we review what has actually happened to industry investment as measured by capital expenditure spending across a sample set of independent oil companies (IOCs) and national oil companies (NOCs).

Higher Crude Prices Impact Demand

By June 2008, the average U.S. consumer kept driving despite the fact that gasoline prices were above the $4-per-gallon mark at the local pump in many areas of the U.S. market. Consumers still needed to commute to work and, for the short term, adjusted personal budgets elsewhere and reduced discretionary spending thereby signaling eminent contraction in many consumer industries.

The most telling statistic associated with peak oil prices was the Department of Energy's (DOE) reported approximate 900,000 bpd crude oil demand drop in the second quarter in 2008. Airline, transport, trucking, and railroad companies all decreased jet fuel and distillate (NYMEX heating oil no. 2) fuel use. When commercial and industrial users of refined fuels experienced higher operating cost structures they accordingly reacted by cutting schedules, combining payloads, and reducing fuel use any way possible.

After the historic fall of Lehman Brothers and AIG on September 15 and 16, 2008, already tight credit markets froze. One of the most noticeable effects took place in the money markets where the spread between A2P2 issuers and A1P1 issuers jumped to more than 400 basis points. Thirty-day LIBOR rates sky-rocketed to more than 7 percent from near 2 percent levels and institutional investors all but shut down the commercial paper market for A2P2 and asset backed securities (ABS) issuers.

Overnight, short-term financing cost structures for most corporations rose by several hundred basis points to unprecedented levels. This period was undoubtedly every corporate treasurer's nightmare. For almost three weeks, many institutional investors simply stayed on the sidelines. After several weeks, the U.S. government stepped in as the investor of last resort and stabilized the commercial paper markets by buying ABS and A2P2 commercial paper. By then, the damage had already been done and seemingly was irreparable.

Global Oil Imbalance

After consumer and commercial and industrial spending contracted, factory orders and industrial production globally plunged across many key industries such as auto, construction and housing, consumer electronics, and pharmaceuticals, to name a few. By December 2008, crude oil prices had fallen more than $100 per barrel to near $33 per barrel. In five months, crude oil lost 78 percent of its value from its record high level in July 2008.

Figure 15.1 depicts a 1 mmbpd crude oil inventory surplus by the fourth quarter (4Q) of 2008. The unprecedented plunge in crude prices was driven by expectations of a pervasive lack of crude demand among Organization for Economic Cooperation and Development (OECD) countries and considerably diminished demand among emerging market countries.

This crisis illustrated the speed with which the commercial and industrial sector reacts to higher cost structures when commodity prices climbed to unprecedented levels. As the financial crisis unfolded, expectations of decreased future crude demand began to emerge and propelled crude prices down below $40 per barrel.

A frequent question is what exactly drove crude oil prices to historic highs. Was it speculators? The research is clear that there is no smoking gun pointing to speculators. What is evident in the research is a crude oil inventory shortage in the quarters leading up to $147 per barrel and an inventory surplus once crude oil demand began to plummet in the 3Q of 2008 and afterwards. The

FIGURE 15.1 Global Oil Balance Chart

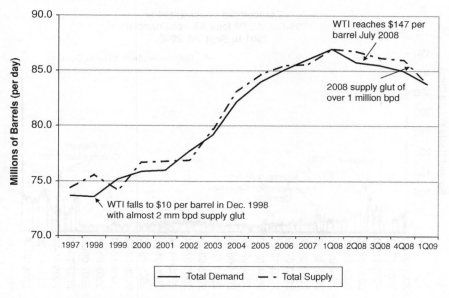

Source: International Energy Agency (IEA).

chart above supports this assertion. By the 4Q of 2008, the Organization of Petroleum Exporting Countries (OPEC) stepped in and began to cut crude oil production by 2.0 to 2.5 mmbpd. This reduction placed a floor under crude oil prices preventing them from dipping below the $30 per barrel level.

Unprecedented Financial Crises

It is important to note that what has been termed the *credit crunch* began in August 2007 when the structured finance market collapsed after the French financial giant, Banque Paribas, said it could not place a value on subprime assets in its portfolio. As a result, credit was already tight in early 2008. Upon the collapse of Lehman and AIG, credit simply dried up for many sub-investment grade corporate borrowers. The high investment-grade companies still had access to credit, albeit at higher prices—for example another 100 to 150 basis points higher. This is high by historical standards for borrowers used to not paying more than a few basis points.

What the financial markets experienced was an economic calamity worse than that of a September 11, 2001-type market shock. Interestingly enough, the spread between A2P2 and AA Nonfinancial issuers in Figure 15.2 depicts that in

FIGURE 15.2   Historic A2P2 Commercial Paper Spread Chart

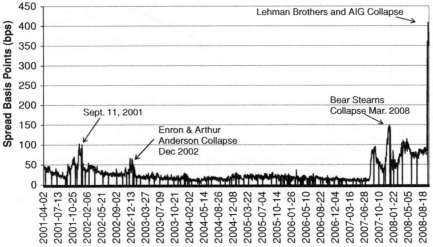

Source: Federal Reserve.

September 2001, the short-term money markets were relatively calm compared to the meltdown the markets experienced on September 15 and 16 of 2008.

Great Commodity Collapse of 2009

The great commodity collapse ensued. The prices of aluminum, iron ore, steel, crude oil, gasoline, jet fuel, and distillates all cratered on expectations of a prolonged global economic slump. Indeed, subsequent economic data revealed that the *Great Recession* began in December 2007 and the latest quarterly data revealed a 6.0 percent annualized contraction in the U.S. gross domestic product (GDP).

In general, integrated majors had record fourth quarter and fiscal year end 2008 earnings due primarily to record high July 2008 West Texas Intermediate (WTI) prices. By the first quarter 2009, the damage had become apparent. Inside a six-month timeframe, virtually across the board, many oil corporations reported 50 percent to 60 percent decreases in net earnings as a result of the plunge in global crude oil prices. Figure 15.3 depicts the dramatic decline of crude oil prices during this time period and its subsequent steady increase. Concurrent with the drop in net earnings across global integrated majors, the oil field service sector companies were also adversely impacted. Integrated majors began the arduous

FIGURE 15.3 Historic WTI Crude Oil Prices Chart ($ per barrel)

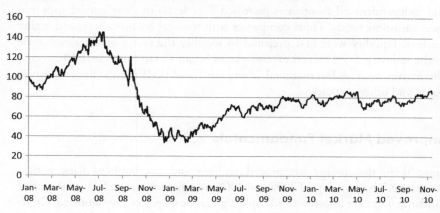

Source: Bloomberg.

task of re-negotiating contracts with oil field service sector firms to attain lower day rates as crude oil demand plummeted. As one would expect, re-negotiating contracts met with much resistance from oil field service companies.

Leverage Creep

First quarter 2009 earnings set the stage for what was arguably the most challenging year the oil and gas sector had seen in the previous five years. The market expected an equally lackluster 2Q 2009 earnings, with crude prices that were on target to post another 56 percent decline below 2Q 2008 levels. With crude oil trading in the $55 to $65 per barrel range, the dramatic collapse in crude oil prices clearly affected both revenues and earnings of global integrated oil majors, resulting in continued project rationalizations.

How quickly and to what extent oil companies can reduce cost structures in the face of what was the steepest earnings decline in five years remained to be seen. While retrenchment in the industry was not expected, project rationalization was the order of the day as marginal, high-cost projects got shelved as companies focused on endeavors with the highest net present value.

Cash-flow pressures began even as the industry struggled to cut costs. In fiscal 2009, leverage creep began to spread throughout the energy value chain. Chapter 3 illustrates the changes in net debt to EBITDA (earnings before interest, taxes, depreciation, and amortization) and total debt to EBITDA between 2006 and 2010. Total debt to EBITDA increased from 1.7x in 2007 to 2.3x in 2009 across a sample set of 1,700 companies in the energy value chain. Similarly, net debt to EBITDA increased from 0.6x in 2007 to 1.2x in 2009.

The amount of corporate leverage began to creep upward as most state-owned and independent oil companies increased debt levels to close budget gaps and meet cash-flow needs. Those companies with stronger balance sheets and higher levels of liquidity were best prepared to weather the storm of the down cycle in the industry. State-owned oil companies began to tap multi-lateral financing alternatives such as International Monetary Fund (IMF), U.S. Export-Import Bank, and other agencies.

Improved Market Fundamentals

Since then, the market has proved resilient and has bounced back with a vengeance. The dark days of 2008 and 2009 are a mere memory. Today, oil-market fundamentals have improved and triple digit crude oil prices have returned. Crude inventories are still relatively high and above their five-year average. However, consumer and industrial demand is slowly increasing in OECD countries, giving a further boost to already strong emerging-market crude demand.

In the United States, a modest economic recovery is unfolding and is generally supportive of a bullish crude market. Backwardation has set briefly into North Sea Brent markets where near-term prices are trading at a higher price than futures contracts many months away. This is indicative of investors willing to pay a premium for barrels in the near-term while prices are expected to decrease in the future. As of this writing, the Brent forward curve is relatively flat, with Brent crude prices over \$122. The reverse of the market situation is a Contango market, in which prices for commodities to be delivered in future months are higher than prices for near-term months. In a Contango market, commodity prices are expected to increase in the future. As of this writing, the WTI crude market is in Contango with crude prices currently over \$110 per barrel and the futures contracts 12 months out for WTI priced near \$110 per barrel. Clearly, the crude oil market has returned.

Investment Outlook

What does the investment outlook appear to be now that a moderate economic recovery has set in? To answer this question and assess the near-term outlook, we analyzed a sample consisting of 20 integrated majors that are either an IOC, NOC, a hybrid-capitalized oil company, or a mid-sized independent oil company. All companies were analyzed for capital expenditure programs between 2006 and 2010 as measured in U.S. dollars. These companies are representative of North American, South American, Western European, and Russian oil companies. Fiscal 2010 data is the last 12 months as of September 30, 2010 (LTM 2010).

The results were surprising. Capital expenditure programs of large-cap firms such as IOCs and NOCs, and mid-sized independents firms were unaffected by

FIGURE 15.4 Capital Investment Chart

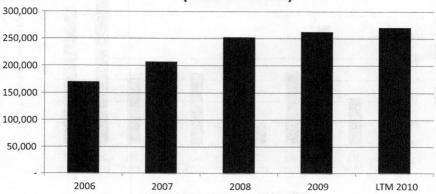

Capital Expenditure Spending ($MM) (2006-LTM 2010)

Source: Analytics provided by Brookshire Advisory and Research, Inc. Copyright © Capital IQ, Inc, a Standard & Poor's business. Standard & Poor's including its subsidiary corporations is a division of The McGraw Hill Companies, Inc. Reproduction of this Chart in any form is prohibited without Capital IQ, Inc.'s prior written permission.

the economic downturn in the commodity cycle. The large-cap firms kept their capital expenditure programs intact. Individual projects were subject to delay. Lower margin projects were put on the back burner until commodity prices bounced back. However, investment spending continued uninterrupted.

Our sample did not include oil juniors. Certainly, small-cap firms such as oil juniors were adversely affected by the downturn. Many of these firms simply idled their drill rig activity until crude oil or natural gas prices returned to more palatable levels. The chart in Figure 15.4 illustrates continuous growth in capital spending among the largest IOCs and NOCs. Keep in mind that the chart in Figure 15.5 isn't measuring drill rig activity or the like. Figure 15.5 illustrates the resilience of the energy industry as commodity prices began to rebound from the downturn in the cycle in early 2009. Total deal size of energy-related transactions includes merger, acquisition, and divestiture activity for the entire energy value chain. As crude oil prices began their ascent in the fourth quarter of 2009 so did merger and acquisition activity.

Concluding Thoughts

The period from 2008 to 2009 represents a historic period in the crude oil industry. Never before has the industry witnessed the top of the commodity cycle and the bottom within two quarters. What is evident is that commercial users

FIGURE 15.5   Total Energy Transaction versus Crude Oil Price Chart

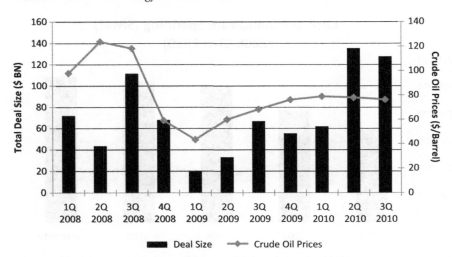

Deal Size ■■■   Crude Oil Prices ◆

of fuels react to increases in commodity prices as it adversely affects their cost structures. Commercial users such as airlines and transport companies will begin to retrench as fuel costs increase.

Among oil producers, Figures 15.4 and 15.5 illustrate the industry's capital expenditure and investment plans are not as easily taken off track with the downturn in the commodity cycle. According to Figure 15.5, merger and acquisition activity slowed down, but picked back up after crude prices rebounded. However, oil producer's capital investment plans stayed intact as depicted in Figure 15.4. Oil-producing companies did not decrease capital spending as crude oil prices declined. Small- and mid-cap companies did decrease spending, and many halted drilling until the economics improved.

PART III

The Power Sector

145

CHAPTER 16

Hydroelectric Power

Part III, The Power Sector, reviews some of the challenges associated with and the progress made in the growth in renewable energy. We explore hydroelectric power, solar energy, geothermal energy, and wind energy. Within the renewable power sector, hydroelectric power is the most widely utilized renewable energy. However, in recent years, many countries have made great strides in implementing wind and solar electric power.

We review geothermal energy and its progress in Chapter 18. Geothermal electricity is not, by any means, in its infancy. The biggest challenge is availability. Geothermal power generation exists in locations that have or had dormant volcanic activity and in areas prone to earthquakes. The challenge becomes how to harness this potential energy and the costs associated with doing so. Here, we review the progress in the northern California electricity market in the United States and the growth in the Philippines market. Both are among the largest producers of geothermal electricity generation.

With the exception of hydroelectric power, the other forms of renewable energy such as solar and wind energy are still very much in their infancy. Hydroelectric power plants have been in operation since the late 1800s with the construction of the Niagara Falls power station in the United States and other small hydroelectric plants in England. Since then, growth in hydro power has proliferated in Asia and South America. We will look at both China and Brazil which are large producers of hydroelectricity. In terms of new hydro projects and investment opportunities, China is at the forefront of hydro projects on the drawing board.

In this part of the book, we also review the status of nuclear energy and developments in this arena. In terms of installed capacity, the United States and France are the biggest producers of nuclear energy. We will review issues associated with nuclear energy as well as some of the benefits in both of these markets.

Renewable energy consists of electricity that is generated from solar, hydro, wind, biomass, and geothermal sources. The largest producers of renewable energy

TABLE 16.1 Total Renewable Electricity Generation by Country (billion kilowatthours)

Country	2005	2006	2007	2008	2009
China	397.3	437.5	437.7	537.3	576.9
United States	370.5	398.7	365.0	392.7	424.3
Canada	370.2	362.5	377.9	390.4	374.5
Brazil	348.3	360.1	387.8	385.2	409.8
Russia	173.9	174.7	177.6	166.0	165.1
Norway	135.2	119.2	133.6	139.5	126.2
India	108.8	122.7	132.5	128.1	121.8
Japan	102.8	114.6	102.4	104.0	98.8
Countries Comprising Africa	91.8	92.9	96.2	97.6	NA
Germany	62.2	71.3	89.0	91.3	97.4
Venezuela	74.3	81.3	83.0	86.7	85.8

Source: U.S. Energy Information Administration (EIA).

are China, Brazil, Canada, United States, and Russia. Please refer to Table 16.1 for the largest producers for renewable electricity-based power generation.

Advantages

Hydroelectric power offers numerous advantages over other forms of power generation. Foremost among the advantages is the cost structure and beneficial economics. Hydroelectricity is one of the most economical electricity sources.

Hydro power alleviates the need to purchase expensive fossil fuels such as crude oil, natural gas, or coal. Hydroelectric power-generation plants can utilize run-of-the-river structures, hydro dam structures, or reservoir storage (pumped storage) to generate electricity. Some of the largest hydroelectricity plants in the world utilize dams such as Three Gorges Dam, Itaipu Dam, and Guri Dam. Hydro power generation plants are less susceptible to operational cost increases and immune from volatility in commodity prices.

Other advantages associated with hydro power include minimal emissions of carbon and other contaminants into the atmosphere. Countries such as China are recognizing the importance of expanding their energy matrices to include renewable energy such as wind and hydro power.

Of course there are other benefits from hydro power plant construction. These benefits include local job creation, improvements in living standards, and perhaps irrigation benefits to agricultural communities.

Disadvantages

The construction of hydro generation power plants may often be associated with the displacement of local citizenry and redeployment of land. Not surprisingly, this is often met with resistance and is a complicating element of the planning and construction process for project sponsors and regulators. In addition, there are the obvious environmental impacts associated with the construction process of building a large dam and the creation of its reservoir.

It is imperative that project sponsors work with local constituents. The relocation of indigenous people, flora, and fauna increases the project's complexities. The social and economic benefits derived from existing resource utilization may outweigh the advantages of locally generated power.

The chart in Table 16.2 identifies those countries with the most significant portion of hydro-based electricity as part of their respective energy matrices. These countries also are the largest producers of renewable energy. The reason is simple. Hydroelectricity is still the single-largest portion of renewable electricity generation.

TABLE 16.2 Total Hydro-Electricity Generation by Country (billion kilowatthours)

Country	2005	2006	2007	2008	2009
China	393	431	430	522	549
Brazil	334	345	370	366	387
Canada	360	352	367	379	363
United States	270	289	248	255	272
Russia	171	172	175	163	162
Norway	134	118	132	138	125
India	101	113	119	113	104
Venezuela	74	81	83	87	86

Source: U.S. Energy Information Administration (EIA).

China

China undoubtedly is one of the fastest-growing global markets. During the economic downturn, China's gross domestic product (GDP) remained above five percent according to the China Statistical Yearbook 2009 (www.stats.gov.cn). In recent quarters, China has posted GDP figures in excess of eight percent. Within the emerging market arena, China is one of the best investment stories.

The increase in GDP has resulted in growth of a variety of manufacturing and service industries in China. In addition, the Chinese consumer has newfound wealth resulting in increased purchasing power. Chinese consumers are buying energy-using durable goods and electronics such as cars and appliances. As a result, Chinese energy demand is rapidly growing. Chinese governmental authorities and the energy industry are keenly aware of the necessity to invest in power-generation infrastructure.

According to the Chinese government's web site (www.gov.cn), China has offered numerous incentives to potential energy infrastructure project sponsors in an effort to accelerate renewable energy generation. Under a renewable energy law that took effect on January 1, 2006, China offered tax and financing incentives to project sponsors for renewable energy projects.

China has vast natural resources and is capitalizing on its water resources to spur growth in renewable energy. Today in China there are several large- and medium-sized hydro projects on the drawing board. Of particular note is the building and completion of the Three Gorges Project in China which came on line in 2008. Three Gorges has an installed capacity of 22,500 MWe of electricity making it one of the world's largest hydroelectric plants.

While coal-based power generation is still very prevalent, to augment its growing energy demand government authorities are incentivizing renewable energy project sponsors. According to China Hydroelectric Corporation (www.chinahydroelectric.com), "hydroelectric power, as a renewable energy, has been granted the highest priority for power dispatches by the PRC (Peoples Republic of China) central government. In the dispatch sequence, hydroelectric power comes after solar and before nuclear power, coal-fired power, and oil-fired power."

Increasingly, hydroelectric power is gaining traction in China. China Hydro-electric also says that in the future China is considering "paying the same tariff to all electricity producers on the same grid." The company further anticipates that ". . . tariffs for hydroelectric power in China should be expected to rise to reach the same levels as that of thermal power."

According to the China Institute of Water Resources and Hydropower Research (www.iwhr.com), China has, across several provinces, numerous hydro projects in various stages of construction or recent completion including the Xiaowan Hydropower Station and the Chu Linh-Coe San hydroelectric project.

TABLE 16.3 China Total Energy Consumption (100 million kwh)

Output	1990	1995	2000	2005	2007
Hydropower	1267	1905	2224	3970	4853
Thermal	4945	8043	11142	20473	27229
Nuclear	0	128	167	531	621
Imports	19	6	16	50	43
Exports	1	60	99	112	146

Source: China Statistical Yearbook 2009.

In addition, Chinese authorities are in the process of constructing the new Sanmen Nuclear Power Plant as well as wind-based energy-generation projects. Overall, China has numerous investment opportunities not only in renewable energy, such as hydroelectric power and wind-based power, but nuclear power plants. China is one of the few countries constructing nuclear electric power generation projects.

Table 16.3 illustrates the significant increase in electricity consumption. Hydro power is still a small, but growing percentage of the total energy matrix. China is still very much reliant on thermal-based electricity generation most notably coal-fired electricity generation.

Brazil and Paraguay

There is no doubt that economic growth in Brazil in the past decade has led to increased energy consumption. Brazil is a leader in the production of hydro-based electric power generation. According to the *BP Statistical Review of World Energy June 2010*, Brazil was the second largest producer, behind China, of electricity from hydro-based power generation.

Brazil and Paraguay's Itaipu Dam, with installed capacity of 14,000 MWe (or 14 gigawatts (GWe)), is another of the world's largest hydroelectric power stations. Like China's Three Gorges, it provides electricity to millions of people. The Itaipu Dam was built between 1975 and 1991 in a collaborative effort between Paraguay and Brazil on the Parana River. According to the U.S. Geological Survey (USGS), the Itaipu Dam provided 20 percent of Brazil's and 94 percent of Paraguay's energy supply in 2000.

Brazil, Paraguay, Canada, Norway, and Venezuela are some of the very few countries that rely on hydroelectric power generation for most of their electric power generation. Almost 90 percent of the electricity produced by the Itaipu Dam in Paraguay gets exported to neighboring Brazil and Argentina. The Itaipu hydroelectric power plant is so critical to both Brazil and Paraguay that when power was disrupted at Itaipu on November 10, 2009, the blackout affected 55 million residents in the cities of Rio de Janeiro and Sao Paulo and all of Paraguay. Many neighboring states throughout Brazil were affected when storm damage possibly impacted power transmission from Itaipu.

There are other smaller hydroelectric power-generation stations on the drawing board. Many of these energy infrastructure projects are coming under increasing scrutiny because of the need to displace indigenous people near the Amazon and possible flooding associated with construction.

Concluding Thoughts

Like geothermal and wind power generation, hydroelectric power generation is another of Mother Nature's gifts. In the following chapters, we will review the status of wind, geothermal, and solar electricity generation in key markets around the globe. The renewable energy technologies have a very important common element—that is each of these electricity sources is a unique solution to its geography. In the following chapters, we will assess the applicability of geothermal and wind power generation. These renewable energy sources are applicable only to certain geographic locations.

It is incumbent upon private industry and government to cooperate to take advantage of power-producing natural resources. From an investment standpoint, it appears that smaller hydro power projects are more easily passed by local regulators than mega endeavors. Smaller hydro plants have a smaller footprint and are less disruptive to local populations. The construction period is far less and costs considerably lower. The smaller projects have a much higher likelihood of obtaining environmental permitting and regulatory approval. This trend appears to be the case in both China and Brazil.

Finally, it is increasingly apparent that growth in GDP and increased energy demand are directly correlated. In emerging market economies like Brazil and China, growing consumer and industrial demand are driving increased need for electricity. As industrial production increases, the living standards for millions are raised. Energy demand is increasing, driven by a population with greater means and the desire to consume.

CHAPTER 17

Nuclear Quagmire

Electricity generated by nuclear energy is an industry encased in regulatory and cost complexities that we identify and analyze in this chapter. We will review issues behind nuclear energy as a fuel source, the future of nuclear energy, and its current status as an investment opportunity.

Nuclear generation plants utilize nuclear fission, a process of splitting apart big atoms into smaller atoms, to produce electricity. The fuel that is used to produce electricity is uranium 235. According to the Department of Energy (DOE), uranium is a rare, non-renewable metal found in rocks primarily in the western United States, that it requires processing before it becomes suitable as a fuel for nuclear reactors.

According to *BP Statistical Review of World Energy June 2010*, 30 countries utilize nuclear-based electricity generation. Nuclear energy is most prevalent in the United States, France, Indonesia, Russia, South Korea, and Germany. These six countries account for 73.2 percent of nuclear energy consumption in 2009. We will review why nuclear energy has proliferated in some countries and not in others and the impact of the March 2011 Japan nuclear crisis.

The Issue: Nuclear Waste

The fundamental issue behind nuclear energy is that of waste storage. Where do nuclear energy generators store the associated nuclear waste? Most nuclear power generators store the radioactive waste on site. There were some industry efforts to store U.S. nuclear waste in a Nevada geologic site. These efforts have not materialized. As one can easily imagine, the waste storage issue and worst-case scenarios brings with it insistence by the citizenry of many municipalities, states, and countries to decrease, not increase, usage of nuclear energy to generate electricity.

Waste storage is not a situation that improves with time; not a lifetime, or generations, or even millennia. Nuclear waste remains radioactive for thousands of years. Furthermore, nuclear waste contaminates everything with which it comes in contact; this includes liquids, which makes for troubling groundwater concerns. Radiation also wreaks havoc with replicating DNA. Radiation poisoning of humans and animals generally is fatal and a particularly undesirable way to expire. Remediation of improper storage contamination is enormously difficult and expensive. These concerns are not going away. Until other storage alternatives are developed, nuclear waste will remain an issue.

On the positive side of the ledger, according to the DOE, electricity-based nuclear generation plants do not generate CO_2 emissions. However, "related activities such as the production of nuclear fuel for reactors do result in CO_2 emissions." The DOE further states, "its nearest competitor in size among non-greenhouse-gas-emitting electricity generating technologies is conventional hydropower, which accounts for approximately 6 percent of U.S. electricity generation."

The Benefits

The most significant benefit associated with nuclear energy is that of cost. When compared to other energy sources, it is one of the most economical fuel sources to generate electricity. The economics compare, on a kilowatt basis, with that of hydro power. This means that it is one of the cheapest forms of energy on the market today.

However, the cost to expand an existing nuclear plant is considerable and increasing every year. There isn't a single power-generation company that is rushing to expand its nuclear-generating capacity. For instance, even if a U.S.-based nuclear power generation company wanted to expand its capacity, it takes approximately 42 months for federal regulators at the Nuclear Regulatory Commission (NRC) to review project applications. Growth in this industry, if one can call it growth, takes place at a snail's pace. Basically, there is no U.S. growth.

From an environmental standpoint, an additional benefit of nuclear energy is the reduced CO_2 emissions from nuclear energy versus other fossil-fuel-based electricity generation. According to the nuclear energy authorities, nuclear energy itself doesn't contribute to greenhouses gases, but related activities may contribute as stated above.

Nuclear Power in the United States

The United States is the first and largest user of nuclear-based electricity generation. Nuclear technology was developed in 1942 by physicists led by Dr. Enrico Fermi at The University of Chicago. The first controlled nuclear chain reaction took place in an experiment conducted in a facility under the football stadium's bleachers. The breakthrough ushered in the nuclear age. Table 17.1 depicts the

TABLE 17.1 Nuclear Power Generation by Country (billion kilowatthours)

Country	2003	2004	2005	2006	2007
United States	764	789	782	787	807
France	419	426	429	428	420
Japan	228	268	290	288	241
Russia	141	137	140	144	152
South Korea	123	124	139	141	144
Germany	157	159	155	159	141

Source: U.S. Energy Information Administration (EIA).

largest users of nuclear power generation by country. The United States, France, and Japan are the largest consumers of nuclear power generation.

In 1957, the first nuclear power plant was constructed in Shippingport, Pennsylvania. The last nuclear power plant constructed in the United States, the Tennessee Valley Authority's Watts Bar 1 nuclear power plant, was completed in 1996. Watts Bar 1 nuclear plant produces 1,170 megawatts (MWe) of electricity.

According to the DOE, there are currently 13 nuclear project applications that have been submitted to the NRC. As previously mentioned, the application review process takes approximately 42 months. The construction process for a nuclear reactor may take another five to seven years.

In the United States, there are 65 power plants in 31 states utilizing 104 reactors to produce electricity. The vast majority of nuclear power plants are east of the Mississippi River, near water sources. Illinois has the most (11) nuclear reactors. The Palo Verde nuclear power plant in Arizona is the largest nuclear plant in the nation, contains three reactors (unit two is the nation's largest electric power unit in terms of capacity), and has a production capacity of nearly four GWe.

The upgrading of existing nuclear power plants to increase electricity-generating capacity is termed *uprates*. According to the DOE, most nuclear power plants are operating at or near their maximum operating capacity. Prior the end of 2008, there were 22 applications to construct new nuclear power reactors on file with the NRC. After the economic downturn in 2009, the NRC received one new application for construction of a nuclear reactor. In 2010, there were no new applications.

Project sponsors, listed in Table 17.2, have submitted applications to the NRC. None of the nuclear-generation infrastructure projects have advanced to the final stages of construction for a variety of reasons.

TABLE 17.2 Status of Potential Commercial Nuclear Reactors in the United States as of April 30, 2010

Site	Sponsor	No. of Units	Capacity (MWe)	Application Submitted
Bell Bend, PA	Penn. Power and Light	1	1,600	10/20/2008
Bellefonte, AL 1 & 2	NuStart Energy, TVA	2	2,470	2/19/2009
Bellefonte, AL 3 & 4	NuStart Energy, TVA	2	2.234	10/30/2007
Calvert Cliffs, MD	UniStar, Nuclear, Constellation	2	1,600	7/13/2007
Comanche Peak, TX	Energy Future Holdings	2	3,400	9/19/2008
Fermi, MI	Detroit Edison Company	1	1,520	9/13/2008
Levy County, FL	Progress Energy	2	2,234	7/30/2008
North Anna, VA	Dominion	1	1,500	11/27/2007
Shearon Harris, NC	Progress Energy	2	2,234	2/19/2008
Turkey Point, FL	Florida Light & Power	2	2,234	6/30/2009
Virgil Summer, SC	Scana Santee Cooper	2	2,234	3/31/2008
Vogtle, GA	Southern Company	2	2,234	3/31/2008
Watts Bar, TN	TVA	1	1,167	7/7/2008
William States Lee, SC	Duke Energy	2	2,234	12/31/2007

Source: U.S. DOE.

Several of the 13 energy infrastructure projects listed above have been mired in regulatory hurdles, cost increases, environmental impact studies, and funding challenges. Since the 2008 to 2009 U.S. economic recession, nuclear energy applications have all but stopped.

Tennessee Valley Authority (TVA) is the closest to building a new reactor. Since the construction of Watts Bar 1 in 1996, TVA has proceeded with the construction of a second nuclear reactor, Watts Bar Unit 2, to meet increasing energy needs in Tennessee. According to the TVA (www.tva.com) web site, the second nuclear reactor project costs approximately $2 billion and is scheduled to come on line in 2013. It remains to be seen whether TVA's Watts Bar 2 nuclear reactor will make it through to final construction.

The Future of Nuclear Energy

Virtually all of the above applications to the NRC were submitted prior to the economic downturn, when sponsors anticipated increasing demand for electricity.

Since then, demand has decreased. However, a modest U.S. economic recovery has not generated renewed interest from project sponsors. According to the DOE, all of the applications in Table 17.2 are still "under review." Given the lengthy, 42-month-long review process and changing market demands for new electric power-generation capacity, nothing will happen quickly.

The construction process for a nuclear reactor itself is north of five years. One can easily envision project cost increases in the middle of the construction process. In most, if not all cases, energy infrastructure project sponsors work with governmental authorities to obtain loan guarantees to back funding of the astronomical costs of construction. Some of the project sponsors are still seeking additional partners to assist in project funding. In other cases, project sponsors beginning construction depends on obtaining government loan guarantees. This is very much a work-in-progress.

Unless there is a more robust economic recovery, it is hard to envision increased interest in nuclear-generating plant construction by project sponsors. Outside of the United States, there may be more interest among emerging market economies looking for more economical energy costs.

From an investment standpoint, we aren't finding many investment opportunities in this arena at this time. We will keep the above projects on our radar and monitor their progress. The lengthy approval process, difficult to obtain environmental permitting, and onerous funding challenges would scare many an investor, but the benefits can't be ignored. Cost-efficient energy is compelling, but maybe not sufficiently compelling in the case of nuclear-based electricity generation.

Nuclear Energy in France

Approximately 75 percent of France's electricity is derived from nuclear-based power generation. Like the United States, France is at the forefront of nuclear technology. What is fascinating is why and how this came to be. After the oil embargo crisis of 1973, France made a national policy decision to obtain energy independence. While France has little fossil fuel resources, France did have technological and engineering expertise in many industries. Building on that strength, in just two decades, France has evolved into a nuclear energy powerhouse. Today, France continues to set the pace in Europe and around the world in what can be achieved in a relatively short time frame given sound energy policy and commitment from its leadership.

Through various policy decisions and legislation, nuclear energy became central to France's energy independence. Today, France has 58 nuclear reactors throughout the country operated by Electricite de France (EdF) as described in Figure 17.1. France has become a net exporter of electricity, providing more than 430 billion kWh per year of electricity used in France, Belgium, Switzerland, Germany, and many other European countries.

FIGURE 17.1   French Nuclear Reactor Map

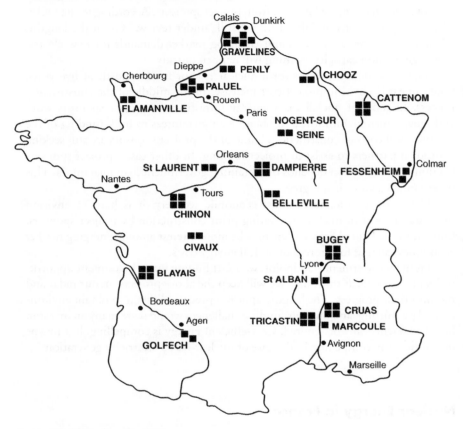

Source: World Nuclear Association.

According to the World Nuclear Association, France's new nuclear energy projects are led by the Commission of Atomic and Alternative Energy (CEA) with a few projects that are currently on the drawing board. EdF is constructing a new 1,750 MWe reactor at the Flamanville, Normandy, plant site that already has two reactors each with 1,300 MWe capacities. The third Flamanville rector is expected to come on line in late 2012 after a 54-month construction period.

The French nuclear regulatory authorities have also begun a program to modify and uprate many nuclear reactors. The modification process has extended the lifetime of many reactors. According to the World Nuclear Association, funding for France's nuclear program was primarily funded by EdF with medium- and long-term debt, bank financing, and support by the French government. The government appears to hold to the view that while building alternative energy forms are important, it will not be become a significant portion of the French energy mix.

Concluding Thoughts

Some of the U.S. nuclear projects referenced earlier are being scaled back in light of increasing construction costs. In some cases, one nuclear reactor, instead of two, is now being considered to reduce construction costs. In addition, project modifications are under consideration depending on the reactor design. In other cases, project sponsors haven't ruled out uprating an existing nuclear plant to expand its current capacity rather than build new construction. One can understand that during the 42-month review process, much can and does happen to change the outlook and viability of many nuclear project structures.

Project financing and environmental permitting appear to be the biggest wildcards. None of these projects will move forward without both. In addition, governmental project loan guarantees are a virtual necessity given the exorbitant costs for nuclear construction. In addition, the Japanese nuclear crisis at the Tepco Nuclear Power plant will prove to be a setback for the nuclear industry. Earthquake and Tsunamis prone geographies have to be seriously considered when evaluating the applicability of nuclear energy. I expect more countries to re-evaluate the role nuclear energy plays in the energy matrix.

In Europe, nuclear-based electricity generation has been slightly decreasing. Aside from France, many European countries are utilizing other methods of electricity generation. Most electricity is being provided by plants using other (primarily fossil) fuels. In addition, many European countries are expanding their energy matrix to include renewable forms of energy where feasible. The benefits of nuclear energy are compelling, but the economics less so. For investment opportunities, we look to a small handful of U.S. and French companies that are exporting nuclear technology as being the best way to invest and suggest keeping this sector on the radar for future developments. As of this writing, France does not appear to be dissuaded by the March 2011 Japan nuclear crisis.

CHAPTER 18

Geothermal and Wind Energy

In this chapter, we review two forms of renewable energy: geothermal and wind. Consider geothermal and wind energy as another of nature's gifts. Both geothermal and wind energy have growth potential but are ideal only in certain locales.

According to the U.S. Geological Survey (USGS), geothermal energy "can be harnessed from the Earth's natural heat associated with active volcanoes or geologically young inactive volcanoes still giving off heat at depth. Steam from high-temperature geothermal fluids can be used to drive turbines and generate electrical power..." Geothermal power plants are situated in these geologically active locations and harness this heat energy to produce electricity.

Geothermal energy is most frequently found in countries or locations that have or had volcanic activity. In addition to volcanic activity, movement in the earth's tectonic plates also creates geothermal energy. As such, locations susceptible to earthquake activity tend to produce geothermal fields. This chapter reviews the status of geothermal energy in the United States and the Philippines, which are homes to the largest geothermal power plants and assesses the companies that support this technology.

We also review progress that has been made in the wind energy arena. Prior to 2008, wind turbine installations were growing at a relatively brisk pace. Many projects were dependent on receipt of government subsidies. Certain governments were unable to maintain subsidies, leaving producers with increasing cost structures. We will review countries that have successfully implemented wind farms. See Table 18.1 for top wind-generated electricity producers.

TABLE 18.1   EIA Wind Energy Generation by Country (billion kilowatthours)

Country	2005	2006	2007	2008	2009
Germany	25.9	29.2	37.7	38.5	35.9
Spain	20.1	22.1	26.2	30.6	34.8
China	1.9	3.7	5.4	12.4	25.0
India	6.3	8.3	11.2	13.1	15.3
United Kingdom	2.8	4.0	5.0	6.7	8.1
France	0.9	2.1	3.9	5.4	7.4
Portugal	1.7	2.8	3.8	5.5	7.2
Denmark	6.3	5.8	6.8	6.6	6.4

Source: U.S. Energy Information Administration (EIA).

United States

In the United States, the state of California has the largest geothermal power capacity, with approximately 2,043 megawatts (MWe) of electricity. The largest geothermal field in the world is The Geysers Geothermal Field near Santa Rosa, in northern California. As such, the largest group of geothermal power plants is situated near The Geysers, approximately 70 miles north of San Francisco. The USGS confirms The Geysers produces enough electricity to meet the power demands for two cities the size of San Francisco.

The Geysers geothermal complex is run by the Lake County, California-based Calpine Corporation (NYSE:CPN). According to Calpine (www.calpine.com), it supplies 725,000 kilowatts of reliable base-load electricity to northern California's power grid. Total installed capacity of The Geysers power plant is 2,043 MWe—from 23 plant sites. Calpine's Geysers facility utilizes recycled water and the power plant produces minimal emissions. Calpine Corporation is at the forefront of consistently producing renewable geothermal energy in an environmentally safe and economically sound manner.

Philippines

Next to the United States, the Philippines is the second largest geothermal producer of electricity in the world. According to the Philippines Department of Energy, the Philippines has approximately 1,977 MWe installed capacity driven by geothermal fields that is helping to reduce its dependence on foreign oil and gas. Approximately 610 MWe are managed by government-owned Philippine National Oil Corporation-Energy Development Corporation (PNOC-EDC). The remaining installed capacity is managed by private corporations.

The Philippines estimates it has an additional 2,600 MWe of untapped geothermal electricity generation that can be developed in future years. Geothermal energy generation contributes about 22 percent of the Philippines energy matrix.

Over the years, the Philippine government has instituted a series of incentives aimed at increased investment in the energy infrastructure. According to Presidential Decree No. 1442, known as "An Act to Promote the Exploration and Development of Geothermal Resources," incentives for geothermal project sponsors are as follows:

- Recovery of operating expenses not exceeding 90 percent of the gross value in any year with carry-forward of unrecovered cost
- Service fee of up to 40 percent of the net proceeds
- Exemption from all taxes except income tax
- Exemption from payment of tariff duties and compensating tax on the importation of machinery, equipment, spare parts, and all materials for geothermal operations
- Depreciation of capital equipment over a 10-year period
- Easy repatriation of capital investment and remittance of earnings
- Entry of alien technical and specialized personnel

The Philippines's energy strategy is centered on increase of geothermal energy and investment in power plants to mitigate foreign purchases of fuel. Some challenges it has encountered have been environmental concerns and socio-cultural issues where proposed electricity power plants are unusually close to indigenous vegetation and people. Project managers must devise creative solutions and obtain governmental support to work in what is termed protected areas or ancestral lands.

Wind Generation Energy

Wind-based electricity power generation is increasing in Europe, the United States, and Asia. European installations are at the forefront in terms of the largest wind farms generating the most significant amount of electricity. Like geothermal power generation, wind-based power generation doesn't work in every location. Certain terrains, weather patterns, and bodies of water are more conducive to producing winds substantial enough to spin turbines used to generate electricity.

Wind farms first began with land-based installations in 1970 in the United States. Since then, wind farms have grown markedly to augment many base-load power generation systems. In the United States, wind-based power generation is less than 1 percent of total U.S. power generation. Renewable energy sources comprise 8 percent of total energy matrix and wind-based power generation is 9 percent of the renewable portion.

According to the Department of Energy (DOE), Europe has approximately 805 billion kilowatt hours of wind-based electricity generation. China has 576 billion kilowatt hours of wind-based renewable energy and the United States and Brazil have made similar progress each with installed capacities in the 409 billion kilowatt range in 2009. In Europe, wind farms have gained traction in Denmark, United Kingdom, Norway, Germany, Sweden, Belgium, and a host of other countries. Denmark and its wind-farm growth serves as a good example of the wind energy arena.

Denmark

The Danish Ministry of Climate and Energy set in motion policies to reduce dependence on fossil fuels. Wind energy began as an onshore form of renewable energy originally thought to supplement peak energy demands on the grid. Over the course of two decades, Denmark has made a concerted effort to build the engineering, technology, and infrastructure to construct wind-based power generation.

The Ministry of the Climate and Energy authorized construction of two wind farms, Horns Rev and Rodsand, with installed capacities of 160 MWe and 158 MWe, respectively. Representing two of the largest wind farms constructed at the time, both of these projects are offshore. Horns Rev wind farm currently is operated by both Denmark-based Dong Energy and Sweden-based Vattenfall. According to Dong Energy (www.dongenergy.com), Horns Rev was constructed in the summer 2002 and is located 14 to 20 kilometers off the west coast of Denmark in the North Sea.

Offshore wind farms have an advantage over onshore wind farms. According to Dong Energy, the output from offshore installations is up to 50 percent higher than for comparable turbines on land. The Horns Rev wind farm is located offshore in water depths between 5 and 15 meters. The visual impact at the shore is minimized by the distance. Today, environmental permitting is becoming increasingly more challenging for wind power-generation companies. While wind turbines do not emit CO_2 emissions, wind turbines do generate noise, resulting in many communities reluctant to embrace the technology.

According to Dong Energy, wind turbine manufacturers are continually improving the underlying technology of turbines, foundations, operational controls, and systems management. An additional wind farm, Horns Rev 2, was constructed between 2008 and 2009 in water depth of 9 to 17 meters in the North Sea off the western coast of Denmark. The price tag was a reported US$1 billion, with an installed capacity of approximately 209 MWe.

United Kingdom

The United Kingdom has a good share of recently developed wind farms. Kent, England is home to the one of the largest offshore wind farms, Thanet, with an installed capacity of 300 MWe. Thanet is approximately seven miles off the southeastern coast of England in a water depth of 20 to 25 meters. The Thanet wind farm was financed under a project finance structure and originally owned by a hedge fund. The project was sold to another investor group, and in 2008 Sweden-based Vattenfall, an energy company, became the project operator. In September 2010, Thanet became operational, making it the largest offshore wind farm.

With even bigger aspirations, the London Array currently under construction will be the largest offshore wind farm at 1,000 MWe of capacity. The London Array offshore wind farm is scheduled to come online by the end of 2012 and upon completion, the London Array will generate electricity for 750,000 homes in the greater London area.

According to the London Array's web site (www.Londonarray.com), phase 1 construction costs are estimated at €2.2 billion. The project will deliver 175 wind turbines, 450 kilometers of cabling, one onshore substation, and other related infrastructure. The London Array is a construction feat as its site is 20 kilometers offshore. The construction and weather conditions are challenging as project builders work in waters 23 meters deep. The prevailing offshore winds at the site are a natural advantage and the technology used is among the most efficient available.

The London Array project sponsors are Denmark-based Dong Energy (50 percent), UK-based E.ON Group (30 percent), and Abu Dhabi-based Masdar (20 percent). Dong Energy has a growing presence in the United Kingdom and currently operates Gunfleet Sands (172 MWe), Burbo Bank (90MWe), and Barrow (90MWe) wind farms.

Concluding Thoughts

In the United States, renewable energy is 8 percent of the total energy matrix consisting of solar, wind, geothermal, biomass, and hydroelectric. To date, geothermal power plants are operating in six U.S. states: Alaska, California, Hawaii, Idaho, Nevada, and Utah. Geothermal represents 5 percent of the total U.S. renewable energy consumption which means, at the present, it is a very small portion of the U.S. energy matrix.

The USGS has quantified electric power generation potential in several U.S. geothermal systems. Its estimate is 9,057 MWe of generation capacity distributed over 13 states. Keep in mind this is potential electricity generation from *identified* sites. The USGS also estimates another 30,033 MWe of potential electricity generation from *undiscovered* U.S. geothermal resources.

Geothermal energy outside of the United States is indeed growing. Since geothermal energy is possible in only certain geographies that had or have volcanic activity, the region also needs to be able to provide sufficient electricity demand and finance the necessary infrastructure. Challenges with energy project infrastructure, including costs, are a prime consideration. Like other power plants, funding, partnerships, environmental permitting, and cost structure play a significant role in construction and plant modification.

Wind energy is slowly gaining in geographies conducive to wind-based electricity generation. In most countries that have wind-based power generation, it is still a relatively small portion of the energy matrix. The benefits from wind energy are zero carbon emissions, however the cost structures are still considerable. Most wind farm sponsors generally are consortiums of three to four companies partnering to develop and finance these projects.

Companies such as Siemens and General Electric have a solid presence in geothermal and wind power-generation equipment. Denmark-based companies such as Dong Energy and Vestas are heavyweights in wind turbine technology and power commercialization.

CHAPTER 19

Solar Energy

Like other forms of renewable energy, solar energy can only be well utilized in certain locations around the globe. As one would expect, geographies that receive intense sunlight for long periods are ideal locations for solar-based power generation. Solar power is increasing in the marketplace, particularly in certain locations in Europe and the United States. In recent years, Spain, Germany, and other countries have been aggressively implementing solar-based power generation. In this chapter, we will review the opportunities and challenges associated with solar-based power generation and look at three distinct markets: Spain, Germany, and the United States. All three countries have adopted and implemented solar-based power generation under slightly different regulatory regimes.

Types of Solar Energy

According to the DOE, there are two primary types of solar energy being produced today:

- Solar Photovoltaic (PV) Cells which change sunlight directly into electricity. Individual PV cells are grouped into panels and arrays of panels that can be used in a wide range of applications . . . including large power plants covering many acres.
- Concentrating Solar Power plants generate electricity by using the heat from solar thermal collectors to heat a fluid which produces steam that is used to power the generator.

Solar photovoltaic panels are arranged in arrays, sometimes over hundreds of acres, to capture the largest amount of energy when the sunlight is most intense. The solar photovoltaic panels are tilted and adjusted to optimize light collection throughout the day. Concentrating solar power plants generally use adjustable

TABLE 19.1   Solar, Tide, and Wave Electricity Generation (billion kilowatthours)

Country	2005	2006	2007	2008	2009
Germany	1.22	2.11	2.92	4.20	5.89
Spain	0.04	0.11	0.48	2.45	5.83
Japan	1.42	1.70	1.91	2.14	2.14
U.S.	0.55	0.51	0.61	0.86	0.81
France	0.52	0.50	0.51	0.53	0.62
S. Korea	0.01	0.03	0.07	0.27	0.95
China	0.09	0.10	0.12	0.21	0.43
Italy	0.03	0.03	0.04	0.18	0.71

Source: U.S. Energy Information Administration (EIA).

mirrors to reflect and concentrate sunlight onto receivers that collect the solar energy and convert it to heat energy.

Due to the variations in sunlight, solar energy power generation can be highly dependent on location, weather, time of day, and time of year. Consequently, many solar-based power plants are utilized as supplementary electricity generators to the primary power sources on the grid.

Countries that have implemented solar energy have done so under different construction and pricing regimes. For instance, Germany and Spain have implemented solar-based power under different regulatory regimes and have experienced different results. Solar-based power generation is still a very small percentage of the energy matrix for most countries. According to the Department of Energy (DOE) (Table 19.1) Germany and Spain generated the most electricity from solar energy in 2009.

Spain

Seville, Spain-based Abengoa S.A. is a leader in the development and construction of solar-based power generation. Abengoa exports its technology to many markets around the globe and, according to its web site (www.abengoa.com), has implemented 14 solar-based power generation infrastructure projects. Abengoa's projects include solar photovoltaic, solar power generation (parabolic concentrating solar plants), solar power towers, and other solar structures.

Abengoa's Denver, Colorado-based unit, Abengoa Solar, has recently secured $1.45 billion in project financing for a contract awarded by the Arizona Public

Service Co. (NYSE:PNW) to construct Solana, the world's largest parabolic concentrating solar power plant. Arizona Public Service Co., the state's largest utility, and the DOE recently finalized the 30-year power purchase agreement with Abengoa. The 250 MWe (megawatt electric) solar power plant will have a total price tag of approximately $2 billion. The DOE is providing a loan guarantee in support of the project.

Spain is home to other such projects developed by a variety of other solar power producers. Some of these power producers were smaller and constructed projects based on government subsidies and reduced electricity prices. Once the Spanish sovereign crisis hit and government subsidies were reduced or eliminated, these smaller power producers were left with cost structures that were not sustainable.

Therein lays the danger in over dependence on government subsidies and the like. Energy infrastructure projects must be economically sustainable and profitable through the life of the project irrespective of government subsidies.

Export of solar-power generation technology is on the increase. Given its desert-like conditions for much of the year, it is not surprising that many Spanish and German solar power producers have identified Arizona as a key market for solar technology.

Arizona, United States

In Arizona, utilities are increasingly implementing solar parks to take advantage of the intense sunlight characteristic of Arizona's desert climate. As mentioned previously, Abengoa Solar is constructing Solana, the largest solar power plant. Utilizing a solar park of parabolic mirrors, the plant will be able to generate 250 MWe of electricity. Unlike solar photovoltaic panels, which utilize the sun's light to directly create electricity, concentrating solar power plants capture the sun's heat with large arrays of parabolic mirrors. In addition, because the process utilizes a heat transfer fluid, concentrating solar power has storage capabilities making the plant operational even when the sky is overcast, the sun is low in the sky, or night has fallen.

According to Solana, "... parabolic mirrors focus the sun's heat on a heat transfer fluid. The fluid can reach a temperature of 735°F (390°C). To produce electricity, the hot fluid transfers its heat energy to water, creating steam. The steam is then used to run conventional steam turbines. The heat energy in the fluid also can be stored and used at a later time to generate electricity." The Solana power plant will potentially harness the sun's heat for approximately 18 hours per day utilizing parabolic mirrors. The stored heated fluid will be used to heat molten salt in thermos-like tanks which can be released later in the day after the sun has set.

For utility-scale project sponsors such as Abengoa and other entities implementing renewable energy systems, the State of Arizona and the United

States federal government have instituted a variety of incentives including corporate tax incentives (such as tax credits, deductions, and rebates). Other incentives include accelerated corporate depreciation, corporate exemptions, renewable energy grants, federal loan guarantees, and renewable energy bonds. While not a comprehensive list, some federal incentives identified by the DOE are:

- Accelerated Corporate Depreciation and Bonus Depreciation
- Corporate Exemptions
- Research and Development Incentives
- Corporate Tax Credit
  - Business Energy Investment Tax Credit (ITC)
  - Renewable Electricity Production Tax Credit (PTC)
- Federal Grant Program
  - U.S. Department of Treasury—Renewable Energy Grants
  - U.S. Department of Agriculture (USDA)—High Energy Cost Grant Program
  - USDA—Rural Energy for America Program (REAP) Grants
- Federal Loan Program
  - Clean Renewable Energy Bonds (CREBs)
  - Qualified Energy Conservation Bonds (QECBs)
  - U.S. Department of Energy—Loan Guarantee Program
  - USDA—Rural Energy for America Program (REAP) Loan Guarantees

Germany

Many sovereigns have provided a variety of economic incentives to encourage building of solar photovoltaic or solar-powered utility parks to augment the primary grid. Germany is among those Organization for Economic Co-operation and Development (OECD) countries actively promoting renewable energy alternatives. In the German market, various incentives were provided to project sponsors for implementation of solar-based power generation under the German Renewables Energy Act. To date, Germany is the global leader in implementing both concentrating solar and solar photovoltaic power generation systems.

Like Abengoa S.A., Germany-based Solon Corporation has also exported its solar photovoltaic technology to sunny locations in the southwestern part of the United States. Companies such as Solon are actively pursuing the utility-scale project market as they expand solar photovoltaic-based electricity generation to power plants. Many utilities have begun to adopt this technology to supplement the primary power grid during daytime hours.

Sulzemoos, Germany-based Phoenix Solar (www.phoenixsolar.com) commissioned and recently released the findings of an independent study conducted by A.T. Kearney, a global management consulting company. The study titled,

The True Value of Photovolatics for Germany[*], assessed the various economic and operational impacts of solar photovoltaic power generation on the German electricity market. The November 3, 2010, Phoenix Solar press release detailed the findings, and the first three points from the study's press release can be summarized as follows:

1. Photovoltaic power generation should be compared on the same production parameters as that of coal- and natural gas-based power generation.
2. When properly compared, photovoltaic power generation is expected to break even in the German market in 2010.
3. In the next five to eight years, photovoltaic power generation will be competitive with other forms of electricity.

What is key here is that A.T. Kearney believes that solar photovoltaic power generation costs, on a cents-per-kilowatt-hour basis, are anticipated to decline over the next several years and become competitive with that of natural gas and coal power generation.

Concluding Thoughts

Increasingly, utilities are augmenting the primary grid with solar-based power generation. Like wind-based electricity generation, the most significant benefits are the elimination of fuel costs and plant emissions when compared with natural gas- or coal-fired generating plants. The construction costs and environmental permitting process are not nearly as prohibitive as that of nuclear energy. Unlike hydro power or nuclear electricity projects which can easily take five to seven years or more, construction of solar parks takes considerably less time. The construction and engineering process to bring a solar park online may take only a few years. The drawback to this technology is the initial capital outlay required; solar technology is not inexpensive.

Several Spanish and German companies are exporting solar power-generating technologies all over the globe. These companies actively work with project sponsors, hedge funds, private equity funds, and other institutional investors. Energy infrastructure projects and sponsors can take many forms.

Solar energy is being utilized in many other OECD markets besides the ones examined previously. In the United States, despite the fact that solar is less than 1 percent of the energy matrix, we see future growth and opportunity in the solar power generation market as more municipalities adopt this technology as costs decline.

---

[*]The True Value of Photovoltaics for Germany a Study by A.T. Kearney commissioned by Phoenix Solar AG.

Many countries are offering economic incentives and tax breaks to local utilities that adopt this form of renewable energy. The challenge with this strategy remains the ability for governments to continue subsidies during an economic downturn. The most visible example of this strategy gone awry is the subsidies offered smaller utilities in Spain to implement solar-power electricity generation. After the Spanish sovereign crisis began, the government was forced to cut its budget along with the subsidies to power generators, revealing that many project cost structures were completely dependent on governmental subsidies.

Investors are encouraged to carefully evaluate the cost structures of energy infrastructure projects to determine what role government tax breaks and subsidies play. It is critical for investors and project sponsors to assess the impact of loan guarantees, bond financing, and tax incentives over the life of an energy infrastructure project. Investors must be cautious and should be wary of an over-dependence of government subsidies to make the economics work. Project financial structures must remain viable should tax incentives and subsidies be withdrawn.

Overall, I am bullish on both solar photovoltaic and concentrating solar power generation technologies to augment primary grids. While both solar technologies have increasingly wider usage, I anticipate considerable growth potential lies in concentrating solar power generation. The energy-storage capabilities associated with this technology enable a smoothing of output and longer hours of operation. These attributes makes this renewable energy source more versatile, which may provide for wider applicability. It is at least a point of competitive differentiation over the solar photovoltaic generation. In the end, market needs and cost per kilowatt hour will enable project sponsors to decide upon the right technology for a given situation.

PART IV

Green Energy

Alternative and Renewable Energy Investments

CHAPTER 20

Biofuels and Ethanol

This chapter reviews the market developments in both biofuels and ethanol markets. In the United States, the ethanol market is dominated by use of corn to produce this alternative fuel. In North America, these alternative fuels and associated markets are in relative infancy. In a market such as Brazil, the ethanol market is fairly mature. We review Brazil as a case study for the ethanol market.

Biofuels Development

In this section, we review progress in the algae and biomass market. Both algae- and biomass-based fuels are currently in various stages of development. We review two situations with regard to private and publicly funded research for these fascinating fuels. In both cases, cost structures will reign supreme. How can these fuels be commercially produced and competitively priced with fossil fuels? That is the imminent challenge.

Algae Biofuels

There are a few high-tech research firms that are actively researching the development of growing and harvesting algae into biofuels. The technology is based upon creating growth environments similar to its natural ecosystem. Algae grow naturally in ponds and open water. Researchers are re-creating these open pond systems or tubular systems where different strains of algae can grow under varying temperatures and nutrient levels. Scientists can alter variables and growth conditions to produce different strains of algae.

Certain strains of algae secrete oils. In layperson's terms, the molecular structures of the oils are similar to that of gasoline and diesel fuels. The idea is to create a biofuel that can utilize existing energy infrastructure. As such, a select group of high-tech research firms have partnered with a few large integrated majors in an effort to commercially develop algae-based biofuels.

Benefits of Algae

One of the most significant benefits of algae-based biofuels is that it is not competing with land for food usage as does corn-based ethanol. Algae can be grown in greenhouse-type environments to meet certain specifications. This is still very much in the research and development stage. Land that is unfit for farming might be quite suitable for growing algae.

According to an ExxonMobil case study on algae biofuels (source: www.exxonmobil.com), "select species of algae produce bio-oils through the natural process of photosynthesis—requiring only sunlight, water, and carbon dioxide." Scientists isolate, test, and re-create growth conditions of select strains of algae, developing those that produce bio-oils with molecular structures similar to that of commercially used fuels.

In addition, ExxonMobil's partnership with La Jolla, California-based Synthetic Genomics, Inc. (source: www.exxonmobil.com) further reports that algae "could yield more than 2000 gallons of fuel per acre per year of production." According to ExxonMobil's case study, approximate yields of other commodities are as shown in Table 20.1.

Based purely on yield, Table 20.1 suggests algae are one of the more promising biofuel feedstocks. One of the keys to algae development is commerciality. According to an ExxonMobil case study, algae may be produced in volumes essential for large-scale commercial development.

Challenges Remain

To date, the economics of biofuels are still challenging. The costs of algae-derived biofuels are still considerably higher than that of conventional petroleum-based fuels. As researchers identify strains with higher yields of bio-oils, harvesting

TABLE 20.1   Approximate Yields of Fuel by Commodity

Commodity	Yield
Algae	2000 gallons per acre per year
Palm	650 gallons per acre per year
Sugarcane	450 gallons per acre per year
Corn	250 gallons per acre per year
Soy	50 gallons per acre per year

Source: www.exxonmobil.com.

improves, and reproduction systems develop, cost structures will begin to emerge and become better defined. Scientists are actively working to determine how to supply carbon dioxide used to grow algae and ultimately integrating it into the existing U.S. pipeline network and refinery system. This aspect of commercial development is critically important if the economic benefit of utilizing existing infrastructure is to take place.

Biomass Biofuels

Various forms of biofuels can be produced from other products such as wood, wood waste, and switchgrass. Scientists at the Department of Energy's (DOE) Argonne National Laboratory in Batavia, Illinois, are researching the development of various species of switchgrass as feedstock in the production of biodiesels. Various species of switchgrass are being researched under a variety of growing conditions on the prairies of Illinois. Table 20.2 illustrates the infancy of biodiesel production around the globe.

Scientists at San Francisco-based Solazyme, Inc. are researching the development of biodiesels using algae to produce commercial-grade diesel and jet fuels. Like algae used to produce other biofuels, scientists producing biodiesel are researching which algae strains are most conducive to producing biodiesel and the optimal growing conditions. This research and development has been under way for several years, but experts in the industry believe commercial development of biodiesel or other biofuels may take up to a decade. Nevertheless, firms such as Solazyme, Synthetic Genomics, and the Argonne National Laboratory are developing and testing these biofuels. Investors, keep these ongoing developments on your radar.

Ethanol Development

In the North American market, ethanol development stems from corn harvest. There is a continuing debate as to whether food should be used as a fuel.

TABLE 20.2 Biodiesel Production (thousands of barrels per day)

Country	2005	2006	2007	2008	2009
Germany	39	70	78	62	51
France	8	12	19	34	41
United States	6	16	32	44	33
Brazil	0	1	7	20	28
Argentina	0	1	8	15	33

Source: U.S. Energy Information Administration (EIA).

Nevertheless, ethanol development in North America is in its relative infancy when compared to a mature and highly developed ethanol market in Brazil. Ethanol use is more prevalent in Brazil than anywhere else in the world today. Why has it proliferated there and is faltering elsewhere? We will examine the economics and infrastructure critical to producing ethanol in Brazil compared to other markets around the globe.

Case Study: Brazil Ethanol

Why has ethanol succeeded in Brazil? Today it is almost impossible to find a Brazilian gasoline station that doesn't carry ethanol for passenger vehicles. In addition, almost all domestically assembled cars are "flex fuel" vehicles. Approximately 90 percent of new car sales are that of flex fuel cars. The used-car market now consists of primarily flex fuel cars. How has Brazil evolved into an ethanol powerhouse? The Brazilian consumer market is virtually independent of gasoline use. Certainly, gasoline is being sold and used but almost exclusively in high-end foreign imports such as BMWs or Audis.

Ethanol Derived from Sugarcane

The Brazilian ethanol market is characterized by the use of sugar as a feedstock for ethanol production. Unlike many other global markets, sugarcane growth is fairly prolific in Brazil. Ample supply of this commodity has helped boost alternative uses of sugarcane for fuel. Sugarcane growth is one of the keys to success in transforming a market. In North American markets, ethanol is produced from corn and competes with the food supply. In Brazil, sugar cane is not competing with the food supply.

Let's not forget that the weather in Brazil is very conducive to sugarcane production. The warm, tropical weather is very supportive of a healthy sugarcane harvest. Rainfall can certainly affect the sugar harvest. However, the Brazilian climate is not subject to severe weather when compared to North American or Western European countries. North American and European countries simply are not blessed with warm, tropical weather for any material portion of the year.

Scale makes a difference. Brazilian market for sugar is considerable. No other commodity market in North America or Europe can produce sugar in the volume that is produced in Brazil. Other Caribbean and Central American countries produce sugarcane, but it is a fraction of the volume that is produced in Brazil. Other major sugarcane producers are India, Colombia, Bolivia, Argentina, El Salvador, Australia, and the United States.

In North American markets, corn is the primary feedstock for ethanol. Certainly, the market dynamics for corn in North America are very different than that of sugarcane in South America. While corn is grown in relatively large volumes in the Midwestern part of the United States, it is not produced in the volume that sugarcane is produced in Brazil. The temperate Brazilian climate permits two harvest seasons for sugarcane. The U.S. growing season and early fall corn harvest are very short when compared to Brazil's dual-harvest sugarcane season. Western Europe has a similarly short growing season. Sugarcane and corn are not the primary commodity products that farms produce in Western Europe.

A Competitive Market

The Brazilian ethanol market is largely a competitive market with numerous sugarcane producers. The producers range from smaller farms to large corporations with significant distribution and production capabilities. The Brazilian government doesn't subsidize the ethanol market to protect its agricultural sector. The ethanol market has to compete based on the merits of the product and the consuming markets demand to buy ethanol-based products.

Flex Fuel Cars in Brazil

Several foreign auto manufacturers have established a Brazilian presence by assembling vehicles that meet local fuel requirements. Japanese manufacturers such as Toyota and Honda, and South Korea's Kia Motors have established a growing presence in Brazil with flex fuel cars. Approximately 90 percent of new cars sales in Brazil are flex fuel vehicles. U.S. manufacturers such as Chevrolet and Ford have also established a Brazilian presence with assembly plants meeting Brazilian fuel requirements. High-end German manufacturers, such as BMW and Audi, have maintained conventional gasoline usage in their Brazilian vehicles. Flex fuel cars are able to run on Brazilian-grade gasoline, ethanol, or a mix of both fuels.

According to Cosan Limited (one of Brazil's largest producers of ethanol), Brazilian-grade ethanol includes: Brazilian Standard Hydrated Ethanol, Anhydrous Carburant Ethanol, and various other grades meeting Brazilian specifications. The anhydrous ethanol is used primarily as an additive. The hydrous ethanol is used an automotive fuel. Brazilian ethanol is different than that used in the U.S. market. The U.S. market consists of the E85 alternative vehicle fuel that contains 85 percent ethanol and 15 percent gasoline.

The Brazilian used car market has also evolved around the flex fuel concept. Today, most used cars have the flex fuel option. Consumers expect and have come to demand the economical driving option. In Brazil, certainly ethanol prices at the pump are a fraction of gasoline prices. It has become increasingly difficult, if not impossible, to sell a used car that does not have the flex fuel feature.

Ethanol Pricing

In Brazil, ethanol pricing is generally competitive. As the largest sugarcane producer, we would expect attractive domestic ethanol prices in Brazil. At local gasoline stations, ethanol prices are approximately 60 percent that of gasoline prices. In the Brazilian market, gasoline prices are very much regulated by the government. In Brazil, gasoline and ethanol prices do not move on a daily basis the way they do in the United States or many European markets. In Brazil, prices for diesel fuels, ethanol, and gasoline are relatively stable at the local retail stations. It's pure economics. Because ethanol is produced and offered at such economical prices relative to imported gasoline, it's no coincidence that Brazil has become an ethanol powerhouse.

Brazilian Ethanol Producers

One of the largest producers of sugarcane is Brazil's Cosan Limited which just entered into a joint venture with Royal Dutch Shell. According to Cosan's financial statements dated September 30, 2010, the 50/50 joint venture with Royal Dutch Shell will be carried out under a Memorandum of Understanding. The relationship has the potential to become a stronghold for global ethanol. Both companies have teamed up to produce and distribute ethanol, conceivably beyond the borders of Brazil. Shell has the global fuel distribution network and made a US$1.6 billion investment (cash contribution) to the joint venture. Investors should keep this situation on their investment radars.

It is important to note that the Brazilian market consists of many large and small producers of sugarcane. As such, there may indeed be future consolidation in the Brazilian ethanol market as smaller producers react to such market moving joint ventures as the Cosan/Royal Dutch Shell initiative. Table 20.3 illustrates the roles both the United States and Brazil play in the ethanol market. Brazil and the United States are, by far, the only sizable markets for ethanol.

The U.S. Ethanol Market

While the United States is the largest producer of ethanol (refer to Table 20.3), the U.S. ethanol market has not reached the scale nor had the significant commercial

TABLE 20.3 Ethanol Production (thousands of barrels per day)

Country	2005	2006	2007	2008	2009
United States	255	317	425	606	713
Brazil	276	306	389	466	450
China	21	24	29	34	37
France	3	5	9	17	22
Germany	3	7	7	10	13

Source: U.S. Energy Information Administration (EIA).

success that is present in Brazil. U.S. ethanol production is derived from corn. As one might expect, the U.S. corn market couldn't be more different than the Brazilian sugarcane market.

As mentioned above, the U.S. Midwest, where most U.S. corn is grown, has considerable weather challenges. The U.S. harvest season is relatively short during the late summer months and soil conditions in the Midwest are much less forgiving. While farmers in the Midwest corn belt can produce significant volumes of corn, other factors may preclude growth of the U.S. ethanol market compared to that of the Brazilian ethanol market.

Subsidies Continue

The evolution of U.S. ethanol begins with a long history of subsidies awarded to producers of ethanol by the U.S. government. As such, producers are generally content to keep producing volumes of ethanol, because the U.S. government subsidizes production and places high tariffs on imports of foreign sugar-based ethanol. According to the DOE, the United States provides refiners with an approximate 45-cent tax credit for every gallon blended with gasoline. Each year, there is a production quota of ethanol and gasoline blend—currently 12 billion gallons. In addition, the United States imposes a 54-cent tariff on Brazilian fuels made from sugarcane. As a result, Brazilian sugar and ethanol have not easily found their way into U.S. markets.

Government subsidies have a tendency to muddy the waters in analyzing the economics of producing ethanol. Over the last several years, ethanol prices have eroded on the heels of increased production. Ethanol prices on the Chicago Board of Trade (CBOT) reached their peak at just above $4.00 per gallon. Once the recession hit in 2008 and domestic fuel demand declined, ethanol prices began to fall. They have since rebounded to the $2.30 per gallon range, but what is evident is an abundance of supply and lackluster demand.

The U.S. Ethanol Commodity Market

At the present, Chicago Mercantile Exchange (CME) trades ethanol futures contracts on both the New York Mercantile Exchange (NYMEX) and the CBOT. According to the CME, CBOT ethanol futures are trading in the $2.40 per gallon range. Gasoline futures are currently trading at a very similar range at $3.20 per gallon. For commercial users, the economics appear comparable. The differences are more pronounced in the production of ethanol, which is subsidized by the U.S. government.

What is concerning is the relatively low level of trading volume for CBOT ethanol. The current front month ethanol contract has a trading volume under 120 contracts compared to the front month contract for Reformulated Blendstock for Oxygenate Blended gasoline (RBOB) with more than 53,000 contracts. Certainly, there is seasonality involved with both contracts. According to the CME, ethanol trading volume has increased more than 200 percent between October 2010 and October 2009. While ethanol trading volume is slowly increasing, it doesn't have nearly the breadth and depth of the RBOB gasoline market.

Concluding Thoughts

While the demand for ethanol will modestly grow, scale will become increasingly important. It is imperative that a market has the refining and pipeline infrastructure that can accommodate ethanol and an automotive industry which produces vehicles that can utilize this fuel. In addition, the corn industry must be able to produce ethanol in the massive volumes necessary to penetrate other global markets, which impact North American corn prices and supplies directed to food, feed, and other markets.

The Brazilian market appears to be rather unique. Is it replicable in other global markets? Temperature and climate are significant competitive advantages. As such, ethanol will likely remain modest as an alternative vehicle fuel in many other markets. Markets such as the United States may utilize corn-based ethanol, but it could take another decade before it reaches even a modest scale.

Today, ethanol is not commercially available in most global markets. In the United States, it is blended with gasoline to create the E85 specification gasoline. Ethanol generally is not the low-production-cost fuel in most markets. The Brazilian sugarcane and automotive markets are the exception; and the ethanol market dynamics of Brazil are not easily transferable.

In addition, auto manufacturers around the globe would have to become active market participants. Existing assembly plants need to be modified to accommodate this alternative vehicle fuel. Just as auto manufacturers are struggling to keep their cost structures in check, investment in alternative fuels may remain on the backburner until different economic incentives emerge.

CHAPTER 21

Cleaner Coal

This chapter reviews recent advances that have been made in the cleansing technology of carbon sequestration in coal-based electricity generation. It appears there is a fundamental oxymoron behind the concept of clean coal. However, research has produced recent advances in what is called *clean coal*-based power generation. Coal has come a long way. There are indeed developments in this abundant fuel source worthy of any savvy investor's attention. In this chapter, we review coal's production, consumption, and cleansing technology, and finally the future of a cleaner coal. Rather than clean coal, we prefer to use the term *cleaner coal* reflecting improvements being made to reduce carbon emissions. The cleansing technology behind carbon sequestration is still relatively young and not widely employed.

Coal as a Fuel Source

One may view coal with mixed opinions. It is an abundant fuel source which is relatively economical when compared to other fossil fuel alternatives such as oil or natural gas. However, coal is a substance that, when burned, does emit some of the highest levels of carbon and other contaminants into the atmosphere. Therein lays the challenge in the energy industry. How does it utilize an abundant natural resource while managing goals of reducing atmospheric carbon emissions? Certainly, the United States and China are large coal consumers. This challenge becomes exacerbated when one extrapolates coal usage around the globe. Overall coal usage is declining in North America and Europe due to the concerted efforts to reduce carbon emissions. However, coal usage is exploding in Asia and Pacific-Rim countries.

Production

According to the *BP Statistical Review of World Energy June 2010*, coal production has increased 53.6 percent from 1999 to 2009 where global production increased from 2,224.6 million metric tons of oil equivalent to 3,408.6 million metric tons of oil equivalent. While there is an effort to reduce carbon emissions, coal production is as robust as ever. This situation convinces me that coal isn't going away anytime soon. What does come into consideration with many alternative energy solutions is the current gas situation in North America. Natural gas prices are so low that natural gas has quickly become one of the more competitive and sought-after energy sources. When compared to wind, solar, or clean coal, natural gas still comes up a winner.

The largest coal producers in 2009 were China, the United States, Australia, India, and Indonesia. According to *BP Statistical Review of World Energy June 2010*, Asia Pacific produced 64.9 percent of 2009 total global production of coal. China produced 1,553 million metric tons of oil equivalent of coal or 45.6 percent of total global production in 2009. The U.S. produced 540 million metric tons of oil equivalent of coal or 15.8 percent of total 2009 production. Collectively, the United States and China contributed to 61.4 percent of total 2009 coal production. Figure 21.1 illustrates that the Asia Pacific region, notably China, is still a significant producer of coal. The 2009 Asia Pacific coal production growth reflects the emerging market growth in many Asian markets.

According to the Department of Energy (DOE), 31.8 percent of 2009 U.S. coal production emanates from the Central Appalachian region. Other key

FIGURE 21.1 Global Coal Production 1999 vs. 2009 (million tonnes oil equivalent)

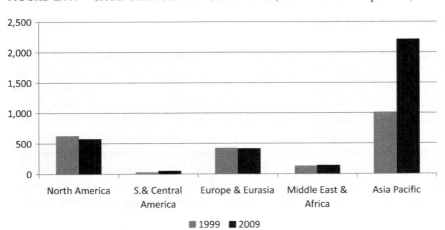

Source: BP Statistical Review of World Energy June 2010.

producing regions in the United States are the Northern Appalachian region and the Illinois Basin. The economic downturn in the fourth quarter of 2008 and early 2009 resulted in a decline in U.S. coal production as demand faltered. Coal demand very much mirrored demand in other fossil fuels. Since then, demand has increased, but not to pre-2008 levels.

Coal Market

Prices in the U.S. coal commodity market reflect the demand picture. Central and North Appalachia prices peaked in mid-2008 concurrent with crude oil prices and then proceeded to plummet in the third quarter of 2008. Once the U.S. economic recovery gained a foothold in early 2009, coal prices began to rebound. However, U.S. coal prices are still at pre-2008 levels. Coal prices for Illinois Basin, Powder River Basin, and Uinta Basin coals are still relatively lackluster when compared to the somewhat cleaner (lower sulfur content) North and Central Appalachia coals. This means that as a fuel source, coal generally is still one of the best games in town because it is abundant and relatively affordable to commercial users.

Reserves

Like crude oil reserves, coal supply is measured in reserves. Coal reserves are held to similar geologic and engineering reporting criteria. Recoverable reserves are those quantities of coal which can be extracted under existing economic and operating conditions. Unlike crude oil, there is an abundant supply of global coal reserves. However, according to the June 2010 *BP Statistical Review*, five countries hold 78.1 percent of total coal reserves. The chart in Table 21.1 presents reserves and reserves-to-production ratios that gives an indication of how long the fuel source could be relied upon at current production rates.

Coal Consumption

The U.S. Energy Information Administration (EIA) estimates that by 2020 and 2035, the electricity sector will continue to be the largest consumer of coal. While the electricity sector's share is expected to decrease to 40 percent by 2020, it is projected to increase to 43 percent by 2035 (see Table 21.2). It is arguably difficult to ascertain future demand. What is clear is the demand for coal is very resilient despite all of the global efforts to decrease its use.

According to Table 21.2, industrial sector consumption is projected to remain fairly stable. Today, it is difficult to project where or how clean coal technology plays in future coal consumption. The cost of installing clean coal technology to upgrade coal-generation plants will play a significant role. To offset the costs, many

TABLE 21.1 Coal Proved Reserves at 2009 (million tonnes)

Country	Total	Share of Total	R/P Ratio (yrs.)
United States	238,308	28.9%	245
Russia	157,010	19.0%	>500 years
China	114,500	13.9%	38
Australia	76,200	9.2%	186
India	58,600	7.1%	105
Other	181,383	21.9%	*
Total	826,001	100.0%	119

Source: BP Statistical Review of World Energy June 2010.
*Varies by country

clean coal technology projects obtain financing through various governmental loan guarantees or other government subsidies. The demand for coal appears to remain robust for the next two decades, with consumption increasing in non-Organization for Economic Cooperation and Development (OECD) Asia Pacific countries as indicated on the chart in Figure 21.2.

Cleaner Coal

We titled this chapter *Cleaner Coal* as opposed to *Clean Coal*, recognizing recent advancements in the technology used to sequester the carbon dioxide in coal-based power generation. There are indeed developments in the technology used to

TABLE 21.2 Coal Share of World Energy Consumption by Sector (%)

Sector	2007	2020	2035
Electricity	43.55	40.10	42.92
Industrial	23.39	22.66	22.02
Other Sectors	2.75	2.39	1.87
Total	26.75	25.82	27.93

Source: U.S. Energy Information Administration (EIA).
Release Date: July 27, 2010

FIGURE 21.2 Non-OECD Coal Consumption by Region (quadrillion Btu)

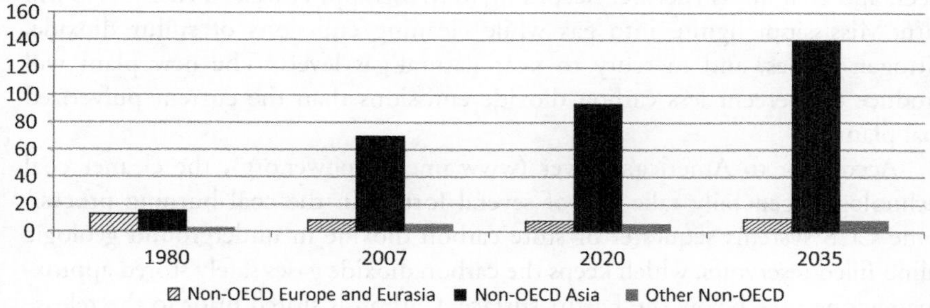

Legend: ▨ Non-OECD Europe and Eurasia ■ Non-OECD Asia ■ Other Non-OECD

Source: U.S. Energy Information Administration (EIA).

reduce carbon emissions from coal. The power generation sector has made inroads in utilizing cleaner coal, but it is still very early in the game. The technology may be utilized outside of the electric power-generation sector to other emitters of carbon. Carbon capture and storage is still in its infancy. The economics still need to be assessed as to whether cleaner coal can compete with natural gas fuel sources—currently at historic lows in pricing. However, progress in cleaner coal technology is indeed promising.

Technology

The developments surrounding cleaner coal lay in technology referred to as carbon capture sequestration (CCS) or the storage of carbon-based gases naturally found in coal. The carbon and sulfur found in coal are generally the biggest contributors to greenhouse gases and atmospheric pollutants. By extracting these gases and storing the carbon dioxide underground, coal-burning power producers can reduce carbon emissions.

Southern Company (NYSE:SO) is partnering with the DOE to develop this and similar forms of CCS technology aimed at reducing carbon emissions. In a December 10, 2010 press release, Southern Company's Mississippi Power subsidiary announced the building of an Integrated Gasification Combined Cycle (IGCC) plant in Kemper County, Mississippi. The US$2.4 billion project utilizes carbon capture technology that according to Mississippi Power aims "to reduce emissions by converting coal or lignite in a synthesis gas that can generate electricity with fewer emissions than pulverized coal power plants."

Mississippi lignite is a low-rank coal abundantly available in Mississippi. The IGCC project utilizes Transport Integrated Gasification (TRIG^{TM}) developed by Southern Company and KBR, a leading global engineering, construction and services company supporting the energy, petrochemicals, government services, and civil infrastructure. According to Mississippi Power, "TRIG^{TM} . . . will turn Mississippi lignite into gas while cleaning emissions of sulfur dioxide, nitrogen oxides, and mercury to near natural-gas levels. The new plant will produce 65 percent less carbon dioxide emissions than the current pulverized coal plants."

According to America's Power (www.americaspower.org), the cleaner coal technologies generally take any of several forms. In the coal burning process, some CCS systems sequester or store carbon dioxide in underground geologic saline-filled reservoirs, which keeps the carbon dioxide gases safely stored approximately one mile below the Earth's surface. Carbon is stored prior to the release of flue gases into the atmosphere. The geologic carbon storage is referred to as Saline Formation.

Other CCS systems store carbon dioxide in depleted oil reservoirs approximately 2,500 feet deep. Carbon dioxide (CO_2) is transported from a power-generation plant via pipeline into mature oil reservoirs. This system is actually a form of enhanced oil recovery and assists in pumping oil, from mature oil reservoirs, to the surface. The end result is coal that has been "cleansed" of its carbon, sulfur, nitrogen oxides, and other contaminants prior to the flue gas being emitted into the atmosphere. The carbon is stored via underground pipelines. Cleaner coal-based power-generation emissions have considerably less contaminants. The chart in Figure 21.3 illustrates CO_2 emissions and their source.

FIGURE 21.3 CO_2 Emissions from the Consumption of Coal (million metric tonnes)

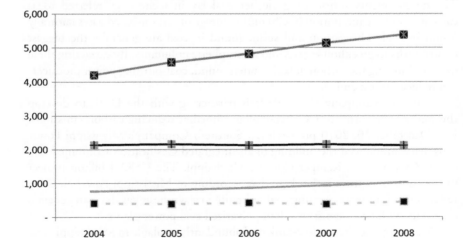

Source: U.S. Energy Information Administration (EIA).

The Economics

Cleaner-coal technology has not yet gained measurable traction in the coal industry. However, as application of this newer technology increases, we believe this has definite investment and growth potential. The wildcard is the cost to implement carbon sequestration technology. Think of this technology as akin to upgrading heavy, high sulfur crudes before these crudes are refined. Cleaner-coal technology is very analogous. Carbon from coal would have to be sequestered before flue gas is emitted into the atmosphere. There are various other technologies that employ scrubbing processes to "upgrade" coal and remove its contaminants.

Cost plays a significant role in cleaner coal. Most clean coal technology that has been implemented in coal-based power generation is a result of government loan guarantees or subsidies. Otherwise, many of these energy infrastructure projects simply wouldn't have made it to first base. The question becomes will government loan guarantees continue? If not, is there availability of private level financing and at what price?

The other consideration is the advances in unconventional natural gas shales over the next decade. The current low prices in the natural gas market are proving to be difficult competition for alternative forms of energy. As low historic natural gas prices are slowing the progress of many solar and wind projects, this market dynamic will also affect the cost structure for cleaner coal energy infrastructure projects.

Concluding Thoughts

Coal demand will remain robust. There aren't economically attractive fuel source alternatives other than, perhaps, natural gas. Much of the coal demand will emanate from non-OECD countries. OECD countries will continue to reduce use of coal. Future demand will continue to be propelled by emerging-market growth. China and India are still projected to be substantial consumers of coal (see Table 21.3).

TABLE 21.3 Non-OECD Coal Consumption by Region to 2035

Region	2007	2020	2035
Non-OECD Europe/Eurasia	8.69	7.94	9.43
Non-OECD Asia	70.34	93.90	140.29
Other Non-OECD	5.55	5.72	8.22
Total Non-OECD	84.59	107.56	157.93

Source: U.S. Energy Information Administration (EIA).
Release Date July 27, 2010

It is not yet clear to what extent clean coal technology will penetrate the coal-based power-generation industry. The costs of implementing clean-coal systems must be economically viable. With energy infrastructure project costs to upgrade coal-based power generation to clean coal in the US$2 billion range, it is conceivable that many projects could be delayed or withdrawn. Governmental loan guarantees may be a necessity to assemble consortiums willing to finance and construct clean coal energy infrastructure projects.

PART V

Summary and Conclusion

CHAPTER 22

Opportunities and Challenges in Green and Traditional Energies

What does the future hold for energy investors? Expect that dollars will flow to smarter, lower-cost solutions to energy opportunities and growing energy demand. Existing technologies will get cleaner and more efficient as operators attempt to maintain market share when subject to competition. New and green technologies will get cheaper and more reliable as engineers move along the learning curve, striving to lower capital requirements and operating costs and solve other issues that keep energy production costs above established competing technologies. And expect that every now and then a disruptive technology will be developed that might just might change everything—after enough time in these slow-moving energy industries. Energy investors must be opportunistic and able to thoughtfully assess market dynamics and regulatory implications.

Renewable Energy

Among alternative energy initiatives, energy production and storage are among the more significant challenges. Production issues are obvious, the sun doesn't always shine on a photovoltaic panel and the wind doesn't always spin a turbine. With regard to storage, the technology needed to store solar energy from photovoltaic panels or wind-based energy is still not developed. However, considerable inroads have been made in concentrating solar power-generation technologies providing a technological distinction compared with photovoltaic cells and wind energy power generation. The storage capabilities associated with concentrating solar power generation make for possibly wide-spread future market applications.

Such projects may present appealing investment opportunities for investors interested in renewable energy. We believe concentrating solar power generation that stores heat energy is one of the more interesting technological developments in alternative energy. New technologies, possibly even disruptive breakthroughs, may appear at any time, providing energy investors additional incentive to stay abreast of scientific and industry developments.

One of the more significant considerations for investors is awareness of energy infrastructure project cost structures. As an example, Solana, the 250 MW solar-based power generation project structure in Arizona will cost approximately $2 billion. With renewable energy infrastructure projects in the $2 billion range, many project sponsors will require loan guarantees or other forms of governmental support. Countries around the globe from Germany to China have responded and implemented numerous incentives for project sponsors.

These incentives include various tax rebates, accelerated depreciation, research and development incentives, and other enticements. Some countries have offered a subsidized electricity price. There are numerous economic incentive schemes. Investors should be wary of the over reliance on such subsidies as they could abruptly be discontinued. Spain is an example of a country that has had to change or eliminate some renewable energy project subsidies to the demise of some power projects.

Smaller Plants, More Plants?

Given the exorbitant costs of high megawatt-output power plants such as nuclear, hydro, or solar-concentrating power plants, one might expect the industry to adopt strategies of smaller plants rather than mega plants. Smaller plants, regionally distributed, require less financing, have smaller footprints, offer lower engineering and construction costs, and impose less social and environmental impacts. More numerous plants offer a strategic redundancy that national security types opine would reduce the effects of major grid failures such as Brazil's 2010 blackout or plant outages due to accident or hostile intent.

This is playing out in China where the government has adopted this approach with respect to an aggressive hydroelectric plant buildup effort to achieve electric power-generation goals. The Chinese government has concluded that building a number of smaller plants and reservoirs is a more efficient strategy than constructing a smaller number of mega hydro facilities.

While China is constructing solar- and wind-based forms of electricity generation, it is also strategically taking advantage of its vast hydro natural resources. The government has instituted various economic and tax incentives to attract investment in hydro power. More importantly, China is taking steps to secure energy for its growing economy.

Cap and Trade

The concept behind cap and trade began as governmental attempts to reduce the greenhouse gases and carbon emissions in the atmosphere. Several global governments instituted various policies by which participants would commit to reducing their share of carbon emissions into the atmosphere. Industries such as the power, refining, and other heavy industries were identified as large emitters of carbon emissions. Heavy industry and sovereigns that agreed to participate had to make commitments to reduce pollutants into the atmosphere.

A global attempt to reduce carbon emissions was crafted under the United Nation's Kyoto Protocol. This pact consisted of formal guidelines agreed to by member countries to reduce their carbon emissions. Each country was to meet certain goals by defined timeframes. There are challenges associated with this program. European-style cap and trade and the now-defunct Chicago Climate Exchange (CCX) were born out of initiatives like the Kyoto Protocol.

Cap and trade schemes were developed to give heavy industry a venue or organized exchange by which they could buy and sell so-called Renewable Energy Credits (RECs). The primary exchanges that developed to accommodate these trades were the European Climate Exchange and the now-shuttered CCX. The European Climate Exchange (ECX) was launched by CCX in 2005, and is the only exchange operating in the European Union Emissions Trading Scheme.

Demise of the U.S. Exchange

The CCX and ECX were owned since 2006 by Climate Exchange PLC, a publicly traded company listed on the AIM division of the London Stock Exchange. The CCX closed in 2010 due to market illiquidity. The Intercontinental Exchange, Inc. (ICE) acquired the ECX through its April, 2010 purchase of the CCX. ICE operates global futures exchanges, clearing houses, and over-the-counter markets.

ICE expects futures trading in a variety of carbon-linked financial instruments—where the bulk of ECX trading activity occurs—to continue apace. That includes trading in futures and options contracts for E.U. allowances (EUAs) and the carbon offsets credits issued by U.N. organizations, the Certified Emission Reduction futures and options, and Emission Reduction Unit futures.

Notwithstanding recent revelations that question the validity of some of the science behind assertions of manmade climate change, a fundamental challenge to implementation of cap and trade policies is that of measurement. Many scientists are still grappling with the issue of how one accurately measures, by country or industry, carbon or sulfur emissions into the atmosphere. Companies will measure their emissions by the amount of output measured from the ground level. Countries tend to measure emissions at the atmospheric level.

However, the debate continues because a country or company will claim to have reduced emissions by virtue of measuring gains and losses by using different methodologies and a variety of measuring devices and criteria. Market transparency is missing, and that doesn't bode well for the system.

In other words, objective criteria and standardized measurement techniques need to be used uniformly by countries and companies if such a system is to be credible. The absence of these standards is problematic and cap and trade programs have stalled. Some countries and companies are already beginning to reassess the program's premises and validity.

Under the Kyoto Protocol, there isn't any independent objective auditor, so to speak, to take measurements. Each country reports its gains and losses to U.N. climate-control authorities. It appears to have flavors of an honor system of sorts. The system lacks an outside audit feature that is independent, objective, and verifiable.

Even more disconcerting is how does one actually place an economic value on a tradable intangible? RECs are not physical commodities, such as crude oil or gasoline, on which one can actually take delivery. Therein lays the dilemma. Scientists, policy makers, energy producers, and energy consumers are still grappling with how this ultimately will play out. Cap and trade may not be a sufficiently good answer for some market participants—other than the exchange that collects a fee for each trade made.

Natural Gas Opportunities

One of the more significant opportunities in the energy industry today is that of natural gas. Natural gas shales and liquefied natural gas (LNG) offer numerous possibilities all over the globe. LNG is a strategic solution for countries without access to natural gas or that experience shortages. Unconventional natural gas shales represent energy supplies for North America for perhaps a decade. In addition, theses shale plays have the propensity to both meet U.S. domestic demand for the next decade and increase the reserve base for independent oil companies with acreage in the lower 48 states of the United States.

The industry is challenged to continually develop initiatives that are environmentally friendly while meeting the increasingly challenging engineering feats. While unconventional natural gas represents a significant source of future natural gas energy, there are environmental considerations that are under consideration by many regulatory authorities.

Governmental Regulation

In some parts of the globe, government influence reigns supreme over natural gas prices. Natural gas is undoubtedly considered a utility and essential infrastructure in most countries. As such, many governments take steps to limit the increases in natural gas prices. In addition, many governments utilize the opportunity to placate the local electorate and keep natural gas prices in check. In other words, natural gas prices are not permitted to move freely with market forces. The incumbent politicians fear the wrath of citizens at the ballot box. This regulatory policy has very definite implications for natural gas producers and utilities.

What are the effects of such policies? The effects are numerous. For producers, they have little incentive to invest or build infrastructure if they are not able to make an adequate return on their investment. Years of government-influenced pricing will, over time, wreak havoc on energy infrastructure. Examples of such policies are Venezuela and Argentina. Government influence has resulted in the reduction of investment throughout the natural gas and power sector. Venezuela still experiences power outages and brown outs, and is in dire need of increased energy investment.

Offshore Drilling Challenges

The offshore drilling portion of the industry is still being challenged in the United States market by the permitting and regulatory environment. In other countries, the offshore permitting process is functioning in a business-as-usual manner. Most countries, including the United States, are reviewing and overhauling their emergency response systems.

The challenge in the United States is obtaining new deepwater drilling permits under the new regulatory environment. As of this writing, few permits have been issued for deepwater drilling in the United States since the BP oil spill. Shallow water permits in the U.S. market, defined as drilling in 500 feet or less of water, are also slow in coming. While there is no doubt that safety is a foremost consideration, new regulation in the United States is slow in implementation, stiflingly uncompetitive, and not functioning as needed by the industry, its subcontractors, and those who believe that offshore drilling is a national priority.

Concluding Thoughts: Energy Independence—A Strategic Imperative

We close by contemplating the notion of energy independence and its role in national security—for any country or government. To always be dependent on other countries for fuel is not only a weakness, but inherently places a sovereign at an economic disadvantage. This can be viewed on a number of levels, but not only is a sovereign at an economic disadvantage, but a national security disadvantage as well.

In this book, we reviewed countries that made inroads into solving their energy needs. At a minimum, these countries recognized the importance of taking steps to secure their energy needs for the next several decades. The countries profiled such as France, China, Norway, and Brazil made energy a strategic and economic imperative. By placing energy policy front and center, these countries have diminished their vulnerability to price shocks associated with the commodity cycle of crude oil prices or natural gas.

The importance of securing energy is foremost as global crude oil markets reacts to the shocks of Middle East turmoil and uncertainty. The fall of the Egyptian and Tunisian governments, and civil unrest in Libya are stark reminders of the necessity of a sovereign to secure its energy supplies. As crude oil prices escalate to triple digits, the vulnerability of global economies to market shocks associated with geopolitical risk becomes ever present.

Countries must realistically review their domestic energy portfolio and evaluate its strengths, weaknesses, opportunities, and threats. Appropriate diversification can help reduce weaknesses and threats. Many countries have definite needs or gaps in their portfolios that can be filled with alterative or green energy. Wind and solar power are already supplementing electric grids in locations that can utilize these forms of power generation.

Scale and cost become very important considerations for investors in green and traditional energy. While solar and wind parks are increasing around the globe, the price tag of such infrastructure projects are still in the billions of dollars. Investors looking for opportunities in these areas should know that subsidies and other governmental economic incentives may diminish—or go away entirely.

We've seen that renewable energy cannot work in all locations. Power generation such as wind, geothermal, hydro, or solar power work only in locations that are conducive to harnessing that form of renewable energy. Displacement of traditional energy sources will not be rapid. The key to augmenting them appears to be best and most appropriate utilization of natural resources.

Finally, it is our sincere hope that this book placed most investment aspects of energy in a context that both novices and veterans to the industry found useful.

Appendix: Energy Equivalent Conversions

	Million Btu (British thermal units)	Giga (10^9) Joules	TOE (Metric Tons of Oil Equivalent)	TCE (Metric Tons of Coal Equivalent)
Million Btu (British thermal units)	1.00000	0.94782	39.68320	27.77824
Giga (10^9) Joules	1.05506	1.00000	41.86800	29.30760
TOE (Metric Tons of Oil Equivalent)	0.02520	0.02388	1.00000	0.70000
TCE (Metric Tons of Coal Equivalent)	0.03600	0.03412	1.42857	1.00000

Mass Equivalent Conversions

	Short Tons	Kilograms	Metric Tons	Long Tons	Pounds
Short Tons	1.00000	0.00110	1.10231	1.12000	0.00050
Kilograms	907.18470	1.00000	1000.00000	1016.04700	0.45359
Metric Tons	0.90718	0.00100	1.00000	1.01605	0.00045
Long Tons	0.89286	0.00098	0.98421	1.00000	0.00045
Pounds	2000.00000	2.20462	2204.62272	2240.00030	1.00000

Volume Equivalent Conversions

	Barrels	U.S. Gallons	Liters	Cubic Feet	Cubic Meters
Barrels	1.00000	0.02381	0.00629	0.17811	6.28981
U.S. Gallons	42.00000	1.00000	0.26417	7.48049	264.17200
Liters	158.98730	3.78541	1.00000	28.31676	1000.00000
Cubic Feet	5.61460	0.13368	0.03531	1.00000	35.31478
Cubic Meters	0.15899	0.00379	0.00100	0.02832	1.00000

Scale Conversions

Prefix	Kilo-	Mega-	Giga-	Tera-	Peta-
Numerical Equivalent	Thousand (10^3)	Million (10^6)	Billion (10^9)	Trillion (10^{12})	Quadrillion (10^{15})
Also Referred to As			Million Kilo-, Thousand Mega-	Billion Kilo-	

Source: U.S. Energy Information Administration (EIA).

Glossary[*]

Acreage An area, measured in acres, that is subject to ownership or control by those holding total or fractional shares of working interests. Acreage is considered developed when development has been completed. A distinction may be made between "gross" acreage and "net" acreage:

- Gross—All acreage covered by any working interest, regardless of the percentage of ownership in the interest.
- Net—Gross acreage adjusted to reflect the percentage of ownership in the working interest in the acreage.

API gravity American Petroleum Institute measure of specific gravity of crude oil or condensate in degrees. It is an arbitrary scale expressing the gravity or density of liquid petroleum products. The measuring scale is calibrated in terms of degrees API; it is calculated as follows:

$$\text{Degrees API} = (141.5 / \text{sp.gr.}60°\text{F}) - 131.5$$

Using this formula, an oil with a specific gravity of 1.0 (that is the same density as water at 60°F) would have an API gravity of 10.0°API = (141.5 / 1.0) − 131.5.

API The American Petroleum Institute, a trade association.

Barrel A unit of volume equal to 42 U.S. gallons.

Bcf One billion (10^9) cubic feet

Biofuel Liquid fuels and blending components produced from biomass feedstocks, used primarily for transportation.

BOE Barrels of oil equivalent (used internationally)

British thermal unit (Btu) The quantity of heat required to raise the temperature of 1 pound of liquid water by 1 degree Fahrenheit at the temperature at which water has its greatest density (approximately 39 degrees Fahrenheit).

CCS Carbon Capture Sequestration

CFTC Commodity Futures Trading Commission

Crude classifications

- Crude oil is classified or graded according to its measured API gravity into four categories: light, medium, heavy, and extra heavy.

---

[*]Glossary terms are provided by U.S. EIA and the author.

201

- Light crude oil is defined as having an API gravity of 36°API and higher.
- Medium crude oil is defined as having an API gravity between 35°API and 19°API.
- Heavy crude oil is defined as having an API gravity between 18°API and 11°API.
- Extra heavy crude oil is defined with API gravity below 10.0°API.

Crude oil A mixture of hydrocarbons that exists in liquid phase in natural underground reservoirs and remains liquid at atmospheric pressure after passing through surface separating facilities. Depending upon the characteristics of the crude stream, it may also include:

- Small amounts of hydrocarbons that exist in gaseous phase in natural underground reservoirs but are liquid at atmospheric pressure after being recovered from oil-well (casing head) gas in lease separators and are subsequently coming led with the crude stream without being separately measured. Lease condensate recovered as a liquid from natural gas wells in lease or field separation facilities and later mixed into the crude stream is also included
- Small amounts of nonhydrocarbons produced with the oil, such as sulfur and various metals
- Drip gases and liquid hydrocarbons produced from tar sands, oil sands, gilsonite, and oil shale

Liquids produced at natural gas processing plants are excluded. Crude oil is refined to produce a wide array of petroleum products, including heating oils; gasoline, diesel and jet fuels; lubricants; asphalt; ethane, propane, and butane; and many other products used for their energy or chemical content.

DECC U.K. Department of Energy and Climate Change

Diesel fuel A fuel composed of distillates obtained in petroleum-refining operation or blends of such distillates with residual oil used in motor vehicles. The boiling point and specific gravity are higher for diesel fuels than for gasoline.

Distillate fuel oil A general classification for one of the petroleum fractions produced in conventional distillation operations. It includes diesel fuels and fuel oils. Products known as No. 1, No. 2, and No. 4 diesel fuel are used in on-highway diesel engines, such as those in trucks and automobiles, as well as off-highway engines, such as those in railroad locomotives and agricultural machinery. Products known as No. 1, No. 2, and No. 4 fuel oils are used primarily for space heating and electric power generation.

DOE U.S. Department of Energy

EBITDA Earnings before interest, taxes, depreciation, and amortization

EIA U.S. Energy Information Administration, an independent agency within the U.S. Department of Energy that develops surveys, collects energy data, and analyzes and models energy issues. The Agency must meet the requests of Congress, other elements within the Department of Energy, Federal Energy Regulatory Commission, the Executive Branch, its own independent needs, and assist the general public, or other interest groups, without taking a policy position.

EOR Enhanced oil recovery

EPA U.S. Environmental Protection Agency

FERC U.S. Federal Energy Regulatory Commission

Futures market A trade center for quoting prices on contracts for the delivery of a specified quantity of a commodity at a specified time and place in the future.

Gas oil European and Asian designation for No. 2 heating oil and No. 2 diesel fuel.

Gasoline See motor gasoline

Geothermal energy Hot water or steam extracted from geothermal reservoirs in the earth's crust. Water or steam extracted from geothermal reservoirs can be used for geothermal heat pumps, water heating, or electricity generation.

Geothermal plant A plant in which the prime mover is a steam turbine. The turbine is driven either by steam produced from hot water or by natural steam that derives its energy from heat found in rock.

Giga One billion

Gigawatt (GW) One billion watts or one thousand megawatts.

Gigawatt-electric (GWe) One billion watts of electric capacity.

Gigawatthour (GWh) One billion watt-hours.

Henry Hub A pipeline hub on the Louisiana Gulf Coast. It is the delivery point for the natural gas futures contract on the New York Mercantile Exchange (NYMEX).

Hydrocarbon An organic chemical compound of hydrogen and carbon in the gaseous, liquid, or solid phase. The molecular structure of hydrocarbon compounds varies from the simplest (methane, a constituent of natural gas) to the very heavy and very complex.

IOC Independent oil company

Kilowatt (kW) One thousand watts.

Kilowatt-electric (kWe) One thousand watts of electric capacity.

Kilowatthour (kWh) A measure of electricity defined as a unit of work or energy, measured as one kilowatt (1,000 watts) of power expended for one hour. One kWh is equivalent to 3,412 Btu.

Liquefied natural gas (LNG) Natural gas (primarily methane) that has been liquefied by reducing its temperature to −260 degrees Fahrenheit at atmospheric pressure.

M Thousand

MBOED Million barrels of oil equivalent per day

Mcf One thousand cubic feet

Megawatt (MW) One million watts of electricity.

Megawatt electric (MWe) One million watts of electric capacity.

Megawatthour (MWh) One thousand kilowatt-hours or 1 million watt-hours.

Mm Million (10^6)

Mmbbl/d One million (10^6) barrels of oil per day

MmBtu One million (10^6) British thermal units, see Btu.

Mmcf One million (10^6) cubic feet

Motor gasoline (finished) A complex mixture of relatively volatile hydrocarbons with or without small quantities of additives, blended to form a fuel suitable for use in spark-ignition engines. Motor gasoline, as defined in ASTM Specification D 4814 or Federal Specification VV-G-1690C, is characterized as having a boiling range of 122 to 158 degrees Fahrenheit at the 10 percent recovery point to 365 to 374 degrees Fahrenheit at the 90 percent recovery point. Motor gasoline includes conventional gasoline; all types of oxygenated gasoline, including gasohol; and reformulated gasoline, but excludes aviation gasoline. Note: Volumetric data on blending components, such as oxygenates, are not counted in data on finished motor gasoline until the blending components are blended into the gasoline.

NAIC National Association of Insurance Commissioners

Natural gas A gaseous mixture of hydrocarbon compounds, the primary one being methane.

NOC National oil company

NRC Nuclear Regulatory Commission

NYMEX New York Mercantile Exchange

OECD Organization for Economic Cooperation and Development

OPEC Organization of the Petroleum Exporting Countries

P1 Reserves Proved Reserves

P2 Reserves Proved and Probable Reserves

P3 Reserves Proved, Probable, and Possible Reserves

PDVSA Petróleos de Venezuela, S.A., Venezuela's national oil company

PEMEX Petróleos Mexicanos, Mexico's national oil company

Petrobras Petróleo Brasileiro S.A., Brazil's national oil company

RBOB Reformulated blendstock for oxygenate blending is a mixture of motor gasoline blending components intended for blending with oxygenates to produce finished reformulated gasoline.

SEA U.K. Strategic Environmental Assessment

SEC U.S. Securities and Exchange Commission

SPE Society of Petroleum Engineers

Tcf One trillion (1012) cubic feet

Tonne 2,204.6 pounds (equal to the weight of 1,000 kilograms, also known as a metric ton)

TVA Tennessee Valley Authority

USGS U.S. Geological Survey

VLCC Very large crude carrier (oil tanker)

About the Author

Gianna Bern is president of Brookshire Advisory and Research, Inc., a Chicago-based registered investment advisory firm focused on oil and gas investment research and energy commodity risk management. Gianna is an investment advisor and energy analyst with more than 20 years of experience in the energy sector. Brookshire is the publisher of *The Brookshire Energy Weekly Report*, a global oil market outlook and *The Brookshire Energy Series*, company-specific investment research.

Prior to Brookshire, Gianna was a senior director in Fitch Ratings' Latin America Corporate Finance group and was responsible for rating Latin American corporate issuers in the oil, gas, and electric utility sector. Before joining Fitch, Gianna was the credit portfolio manager of a leading commercial lease finance company where she managed a $2.5 billion commercial finance lease portfolio.

Previously, Gianna was a manager of risk management trading at BP Amoco Plc. Before the merger of Amoco Corporation and BP Plc., Gianna was a senior energy analyst at Amoco Oil. Gianna began her career in corporate finance at Continental Bank (now Bank of America). Gianna has a BBA from Illinois Institute of Technology and an MBA from The University of Chicago's Booth School of Business.

Index

Printed and bound by CPI Group (UK) Ltd, Croydon, CR0 4YY

16/04/2025

14658514-0002